"If you've ever trekked to the edge of the Big Island, crossing the sulfurous charcoal cliffs, across the steaming cracked gravel, down past the green shrubs, following the reddish yellow river to the erupting lava percolating into the Pacific Ocean, then maybe, just maybe, you can imagine what it's like to eat one of Beverly Soon Tofu's incredible cauldrons of soon tofu soup. There is nothing like it and I miss it every day. This was my special place of solitude for lunch. There was a ceremony to the meal, a ceremony that defined the 1990's to its closing in 2020. If I close my eyes, I can taste the thick spicy stew and see Monica cooking 12 of them at the same time over viciously bursting open flames with only a pair of pliers in her hand to grab the pot. And in that dream, Uncle Tony Bourdain is still alive, and we are cracking eggs into each other's bubbling bowls, laughing. Welcome to Beverly Soon Tofu."

—ROY CHOI, AUTHOR OF *L.A. SON: MY LIFE, MY CITY, MY FOOD*

"Many of us still miss Beverly Soon Tofu, Monica Lee's revolutionary Koreatown restaurant. For nearly 35 years she sustained Angelenos and in-the-know visitors with her soon tofu chigae, served in nearly a dozen combinations of meats, seafoods, and vegetables and always rushed to the table with its broth boiling volcanically. With this cookbook, Lee and Tien Nguyen, one of L.A.'s most insightful writers on culture and food, show us how to recapture the restaurant's spirit in our own kitchens. Lee's story is extraordinary, and so are her recipes; they illuminate her life far beyond spicy, delicious tofu stew."

—BILL ADDISON, RESTAURANT CRITIC, *THE LOS ANGELES TIMES*

손맛
Sohn-mat

손맛
Sohn-mat

*Recipes and Flavors of
Korean Home Cooking*

Monica Lee
with Tien Nguyen

PHOTOGRAPHER
Rick Poon

Hardie Grant
NORTH AMERICA

Hardie Grant

NORTH AMERICA

Hardie Grant North America
2912 Telegraph Ave
Berkeley, CA 94705

hardiegrantbooks.com

Published in the United States by **Hardie Grant North America,** an imprint of Hardie Grant Publishing Pty Ltd.

Library of Congress Cataloging-in-Publication Data is available upon request.

ISBN: **9781958417034**

ISBN: **9781958417010 (eBook)**

Printed in **China**

Design by **Toni Tajima**

Food Styling by **Diep Tran**

First Edition

For my daughters

Contents

Other Family Favorites

Introduction

When I opened Beverly Soon Tofu in Koreatown in 1986, it was the only restaurant in Los Angeles, and possibly in the United States, to specialize in soon tofu chigae. If you are not familiar with it, soon tofu chigae is a stew made with tofu so soft and delicate that it can be scooped like custard. Served with rice, soon tofu is a bowl of comfort. It feels like home.

In Korean, *soon tofu* translates to "extra-soft tofu," and *chigae* means "stew." You may also see this dish spelled as *sundubu jjigae* or *soondubu jjigae*. In practice, soon tofu chigae is often referred to simply as soon tofu. The context will indicate whether the speaker is referring to the tofu or the stew.

At Beverly Soon Tofu, we made soon tofu chigae in single-serving ttukbaegi, which are earthenware pots that can go directly from the stove to the table, and every customer had the option to choose their fillings and spice level. It was hard work to do that amount of customization for every single order, but for over thirty years, our customers loved our soon tofu. And we were very happy to make our customers very happy.

Beverly Soon Tofu closed in 2020. The pandemic forced our hand. It was hard to say goodbye, but I am so proud of the food we made there. And through this book, I now have another chance to share not only my passion for the craft of cooking but also all that I learned over those thirty-plus years of making food for others. No matter how familiar or unfamiliar you are with Korean food, I hope these recipes will inspire you to cook and to enjoy cooking both for yourself and for your loved ones.

Welcome to Beverly Soon Tofu.

Sohn-mat

Sohn-mat is something that is passed down from generation to generation. It translates to "flavor in the hands." You do not need sohn-mat to be a good cook, but if you have it, it means that you have a natural instinct for flavor, an intuition for cooking. If you have sohn-mat, you probably don't need to measure very much; rather, it's as if your hands know exactly how much more of this or that the dish needs. You might have someone in your family, or perhaps a good friend, who everyone agrees has that special something, that sohn-mat. It might even be you!

In my family, the sohn-mat is strong. My grandmother's aunt was a cook for the royal family in Korea. She prepared grand, elaborate feasts for the king and his court. She passed her sohn-mat down to my grandmother, who also was a great cook. She and my grandfather lived in the countryside outside of Seoul. They regularly hosted Japanese exchange students, so my grandmother often cooked for twenty-five to thirty people at any given time. Huge cooking vessels and fresh vegetables from their garden crowded her kitchen. There was no gas in those days, so to cook, she carefully managed the heat from the fire of her woodburning stove.

I loved visiting my grandmother during my breaks and summer vacations. I loved following her into that kitchen, being at her elbow as she prepared cabbage and other vegetables for kimchi and watching as she cooked up big pots of chigae and assembled bowls of bibimbap.

From a young age, it was clear I had sohn-mat, too. I cooked for my friends, and I could cook for a large group as easily as I could cook for myself. At school, I did very well in home economics and often stayed after class to help my teachers make extra jeon (pancakes) or anything else that needed to be cooked.

Still, it was more practical for me to study nursing than cooking, so I graduated from nursing school in 1976. But the Korea then was different from today, the economy was not thriving, and there were more opportunities abroad. I immigrated to the United States in 1977 and joined some family who were already settled in Los Angeles.

Koreatown at that time was very small, just a few blocks a few miles from downtown Los Angeles, clustered around the intersection of Olympic Boulevard and Vermont Avenue. We lived about thirteen miles farther west, in Santa Monica, but we made the drive to Koreatown to shop and eat at least twice a month. I continued in nursing for a few years before my husband and I took over a small market on the west side of the city. After two armed robberies, though, we moved on.

During that time, I was cooking, too, but at home for family and friends. One dish I made often was soon tofu chigae. This wasn't a dish I ate very

often growing up. In fact, rarely would soon tofu chigae be made at home. It was akin to diner food, a working-class stew found in restaurants. But in Los Angeles, I found I enjoyed cooking it. For one thing, tofu is very nutritious. And I liked that, unlike at restaurants, where there was just one big pot of soon tofu chigae simmering on the stove, I could customize each bowl for everyone at the table. They could choose their own fillings as well as how spicy (or not spicy) they wanted it to be.

My friends urged me to open a restaurant. I did need the income, but a restaurant? I had no experience in restaurant work. And back then, most restaurants served a variety of dishes; there weren't very many dedicated to just one dish. I didn't know if there would be enough people interested in soon tofu to justify a restaurant specializing in just that one dish.

Still, I was drawn to the idea. A restaurant would give me the chance to do what I loved doing: cooking! And especially cooking for others. And if I were going to open a restaurant, I wanted to focus on one thing and to do that one thing very well. And while soon tofu chigae was very easy to find in Korea, here, even in Koreatown, the dish had been overlooked and was rarely found on restaurant menus. If a restaurant did offer it, it would be just one stew with one set of fillings, take it or leave it.

By coincidence, my sister-in-law opened one of the few specialty restaurants at the time, a place that made beef bone soup. I helped out and observed how a restaurant was run. I thought, *Maybe I can do it*.

I went back to South Korea to research soon tofu. Taxi drivers always know the best, most affordable places to eat, so I asked them to take me to their favorite spots. I visited three places and noticed that just as in LA, all three kept their soon tofu in big pots simmering on the stove, ready to be spooned out whenever a customer placed an order. None gave the customer the option to customize their bowl in any way.

The idea for my restaurant was coming together. I would do what I did at home: allow my guests to choose their fillings and their spice level. Each soon tofu would be individually portioned and made to order, because soon tofu is best when made fresh and served while still boiling hot. If you rewarm it, or even just keep it warm on the stove, the silky texture of the tofu and the nuances of the broth are lost. I knew that making soon tofu one by one would take time and require customers to be patient, but I was sure one taste would tell them it was worth the wait. And I thought I could make soon tofu appeal to a broad group of people by keeping it affordable while still using high-quality ingredients.

Before heading back to the United States, I had to source the cooking vessels. If each customer was to have their own soon tofu, I would need a lot of ttukbaegi. I bought a thousand of them and flew back to LA.

Beverly Soon Tofu

The one thing I could not bring back with me from Korea was the soon tofu. Until the Korean manufacturer Pulmuone opened a US branch here in Los Angeles in the early 1990s, soon tofu was not available in Los Angeles. What was available was silken tofu, which was what I used at home. But silken tofu is not quite soft enough; it's an imperfect substitute for soon tofu. For my restaurant, I had to have the right tofu.

My only option, then, was to learn how to make the soon tofu myself. I found one of the only two tofu manufacturers in LA and sat in their office for several hours before I finally convinced them to sell me just their soy milk. I also convinced someone with more than forty years of tofu-making experience to teach me how to make tofu. He had a day job, so scheduling our weekly lessons was always a challenge. Making the tofu itself was an exercise in frustration. I struggled with getting the anticoagulants just right so the tofu would set and achieve a soft texture but not so soft that it would completely fall apart in the stew. For weeks, I threw out gallons and gallons of watery milk. Finally, after almost a month, I made my first successful batch. I could do it.

My restaurant was located on the edge of Koreatown. I considered giving the restaurant a Korean name but decided against it. In a city full of people who spoke different languages, I wanted a name that was familiar to most people. And everyone has heard of Beverly Hills, right? My restaurant happened to be on a street called Beverly Boulevard. It was miles away from Beverly Hills, but, I thought, no matter what language you spoke or where you came from, you would remember the Beverly part of my restaurant's name. (I had the same idea for my adopted English name: the "Monica" comes from Santa Monica.)

The restaurant was small, with just enough room for thirty-five customers. I wanted those customers to feel as if they were sharing a rustic, homestyle meal in the countryside in Korea, so we brought wood from the Northern California town of Redwood City and built the tables and chairs by hand. I did a lot of the sanding and staining myself. The walls were decorated with rice straw, invoking nostalgia among our Korean customers. (Unfortunately, we had to take the straw walls down, because the fire department thought they were a fire hazard.)

I had four soon tofu dishes on my first menu: soon tofu with a combination of beef, oysters, and clams; seafood soon tofu with shrimp, oysters, green mussels, and clams; kimchi soon tofu with pork or beef; and a plain soon tofu with nothing but clouds of soon tofu. Every order came with rice, of course, and freshly made banchan (small side dishes) and kimchi. To drink, there was barley tea.

베버리순두부
SINCE 1986 BEVERLY TOFU HOUSE

초 청 의 말 씀

더웁고 바쁘고 짜증나는 L.A.의 하루 일과입니다.

무언가 재미있는 일이 생겼으면 하는것도 우리 모두의 바램인 것 같읍니다.

여기 자그만하나 고국에서 즐겨 잡수시던 순두부 전문식당을 열게 되었읍니다. 매웁지않은 순두부, 굴 순두부, 조개 순두부, 그리고 고기 순두부 등 여러가지 순두부가 있읍니다.

다음 외식때에는 친구와 함께, 가족과 함께, 정다운 연인과 함께 꼭 들려주세요. 맛과 분위기는 저희가 책임지겠읍니다.

그리고 앞서 개업식을 아래와 같이 하고저하오니 바쁘시더라도 꼭 들려주시고 저희 발전을 위한 좋은 말씀을 많이 부탁 드립니다.

—아   래—

일 시 : 1986년 6월 25일(수요일)
아침 10시~저녁 10시
장 소 : 4653-½ BEVERLY BLVD.
LOS ANGELES, CA 90004
(213) 856-0368

My first day of business was June 25, 1986. Workers from the nearby sewing and textile factories were my first customers. Others followed. The dining room began to get crowded. I was planning to stay open until 9:00 or 10:00 p.m., but we were out of tofu by 8:00. The next day, we sold out again.

And that was it. People liked my soon tofu! I was happy, but those early days were very difficult. Small restaurants like mine operate on very little capital, and making the numbers work was itself an incredible amount of work. The tofu, too, was a challenge. Every morning, I made tofu from 100 to 125 gallons of soy milk, the most I could make in my tiny kitchen. But it often wasn't enough, so I had to make tofu quickly between rushes. Health inspectors, unfamiliar with tofu and Korean cooking in general, often gave me a hard time. I tried my best to educate them. With some relief, I stopped making the tofu after about five years, when I found a local manufacturer who could make the tofu according to my recipe.

I opened a second location in a strip mall in the heart of Koreatown two years later, in 1988. It was slightly bigger and decorated in the same rustic aesthetic as the first. In 1992, I closed the original location. Over the years, we went through thousands of ttukbaegi, and my menu expanded to include even more options for fillings, as well as larger plates like galbi and other meat dishes to share. For many years, most of my customers were Korean or Korean American, but slowly, more non-Koreans started dropping in, too. Linda Burum at the *Los Angeles Times* wrote about us soon after the second location opened in 1988. At the time, Seoul was hosting the summer Olympics, which sparked an interest in Koreatown. Jonathan Gold, the *Los Angeles Times*'s restaurant critic, gave us a nice review in the early 1990s. During that same decade, tofu became part of a big health trend, and we introduced many people to soon tofu. I was told there were celebrities coming in, but I would recognize customers more from their usual orders than from who they were. (I did recognize one famous actor, from the movie *Titanic*. I later learned he was Leonardo DiCaprio.)

Still, despite the media attention and love from customers, there was never any guarantee of success. We could be very busy one week and very slow the next. There were times when I was unsure if the business could continue. Indeed, the days were incredibly long and never seemed to get shorter. I like to select my own produce and talk with the vendors, so I was up every day at 4:00 a.m. to head down to the wholesale market to place my orders. I picked them up a few hours later, then headed to the restaurant to cook and prepare everything before we opened at 9:30 a.m. I worked until we closed at 10:30 p.m.

The turning point, the moment when I finally felt stable, was in 2013, when chefs Anthony Bourdain and Roy Choi came in to film an episode of the CNN series *Parts Unknown*. With that one episode, soon tofu became widely known throughout the United States, introducing my restaurant to a whole new audience who came and celebrated the humble tofu stew. We had visitors from all over the country: Chicago, Texas, Hawaii, New York. I loved it that people loved not just Korean food in Koreatown but also the food I was making. It was the best feeling to make food for others. Everything was going well.

And then came March of 2020.

The Closing

At the beginning of the pandemic, in March of 2020, we closed for six weeks. When we reopened, my daughters CJ and JJ helped me convert Beverly Soon Tofu into a takeout-only operation. We made the best of an extremely uncertain time. But as the months wore on, it was increasingly difficult to keep up with the constantly changing guidelines for restaurant dining. The pandemic was only getting worse. My daughters and I agreed it was not tenable to just barely hold on, and so on September 7, we announced that our last day of service would be September 20.

The response was instant. We were not prepared for the outpouring of support. We were inundated, orders coming in so fast that we had to keep turning our online ordering system off and on to keep up. Customers waited for two or three hours to pick up their meals. Regulars I had come to know over twenty to thirty years dropped by. Some I had first met when they were just kids, and, now in their forties, they came back to share memories. Things were so busy that CJ and JJ stepped away from their day jobs to help, giving me time to say hello and to thank everyone who came to wish us well.

Since Beverly Soon Tofu closed, what I miss most are my customers. They are what made the restaurant so rewarding. "Oh, Monica, the soon tofu was so delicious!" they'd say on their first visit. "I'll be back!" And they would come back, often returning with friends. Beverly Soon Tofu was the first taste of tofu or Korean food for so many, and for others, it was the taste of home. It was where many couples had their first date, and where they returned to celebrate their anniversaries. It was where birthdays, promotions, and other occasions were celebrated. It brought me so much joy to see so many people enjoying my food.

This Cookbook

When I opened Beverly Soon Tofu in 1986, I didn't set out to be a pioneer or a leader in anything. I just had a vision and a love for food, and I especially loved to see people tasting and enjoying the food I made. I believed in hard work and attention to detail, not because I had the luxury of extra time or resources but because I believed in what I cooked. I put in sixteen- to eighteen-hour days and invested everything in this business to make it work. It didn't always, but it wasn't for lack of trying.

Throughout the rough patches, I had fiercely loyal customers who appreciated all the details and effort I put into the restaurant and the countless hours I spent ensuring that everything was just right: seasoning thousands of clay pots every year, personally selecting the produce every morning, and making kimchi and banchan from scratch every day.

Beverly Soon Tofu wasn't just a business to me. It was a passion. And it is that passion that I would like to pass on to all those who use my recipes to make soon tofu chigae and the other dishes in this book.

The recipes I have chosen to include here are those very close to me: recipes for my soon tofu, of course, as well as dishes that accompany the soon tofu, including small side dishes, kimchi, and large protein platters. I also include a few extra dishes, like other types of soups that aren't always served with soon tofu but are personal favorites that I'd love to share with you. Many are recipes I learned from my grandmother. Whether you are new to Korean cooking or you know Korean food well but would like some guidance in the kitchen, this book is for you.

Many of my recipes can be made in an hour or less. With practice, they will come together even faster. Certain dishes will come together in no time at all if you already have some of the foundational broths and bases on hand, so I encourage you to spend the time making those in advance so you can use them throughout the week. And if you spend an afternoon making a few kimchi, your efforts will be rewarded in the long run.

Affordability is very important to me. Most of my recipes are inexpensive to make or can be adapted to fit your budget and to use what you already have in your pantry or fridge. I also offer Spinoffs, which are suggestions for how to use every part of a vegetable, how to stretch ingredients across meals, and how to be creative with leftovers. Nothing is wasted in my kitchen!

The book is divided into a few sections. The Pantry and Shopping Guide offers advice and details about the ingredients and equipment I use most often. Almost everything you need to cook from this book can be found at Korean and other Asian markets. For further shopping advice, refer to Resources (page 238).

From there, I move on to making the soon tofu, starting with a step-by-step guide to the entire process of prepping, cooking, filling, and serving the stew. I recommend reading this guide before making the soon tofu recipes that follow.

Like any Korean meal, soon tofu is usually served with rice, banchan, kimchi, and a larger shared dish or two. The Soon Tofu Table focuses on the banhan and kimchi I like to serve with the stew.

Finally, Other Family Favorites features appetizers, shared platters, and other types of soups that I love to make at home. They take advantage of many of the same ingredients we made or used in the earlier sections, so you do not have to do any extra shopping! Mix and match these dishes with the kimchi and banchan recipes for a full meal.

Many of my recipes are vegetarian, vegan, or gluten-free or can be made so with a few adjustments. Where appropriate, I have indicated whether a recipe meets those dietary needs or how it can be adjusted to do so.

Beyond recipes, I also want to reemphasize the importance of passion. You do not need to have sohn-mat to make delicious food, but you do need to have the *intention* to make delicious food. I believe the feelings you have while making food can be tasted. If you are angry or indifferent while you cook, the food will taste different than when you cook with care and love. Be present when cooking. Think about whom you are cooking for, and you will make wonderful meals.

Beverly Soon Tofu may be closed, but its spirit lives on. I am so happy to have another chance to share my cooking with you. Please enjoy.

Pantry and Shopping Guide

Everything you need to make the dishes in this book can be found at Korean markets. Other Asian markets have most everything, too, though depending on the item, they may not have the depth of selection and variety that you'll find at Korean markets. If you have a local Korean grocer, I encourage you to try it first for your shopping needs.

The following guide includes the items I always have in my kitchen. Use this resource to help you begin building your pantry. This does not include every item used in this cookbook, but it does cover the ingredients and cookware I use the most, along with my advice for shopping, preparation, and storage.

Vegetables

Of the wide variety of vegetables I use in my everyday cooking, the following are the ones I always have in my refrigerator. Korean markets often carry highly seasonal vegetables from Korea that you may not find elsewhere.

CHIVES

Both Korean chives and Chinese chives (also called Asian chives or garlic chives) are used throughout this book. Both have a mildly garlicky flavor, but Korean chives are thinner and shorter than the bigger and longer Chinese chives. Korean chives are also more tender than Chinese chives, making them ideal for delicate dishes and many kimchi. Chinese chives, on the other hand, are perfect for stir-fry dishes like my Grandma's Eggs and Chives (page 109) banchan. Korean chives can be found at Korean and many Asian markets in the spring and summer; look for chives that are at least ¼ inch wide / 6mm. Chinese chives are available year-round and can be substituted for Korean chives when you can't find Korean chives or when the Korean chives are too thin.

GREEN ONIONS

Green onions are a big part of my cooking, so much so that no matter how many bunches I have in my refrigerator, I can never pass up the chance to pick up another bunch that look especially green and fresh. Korean markets have a large selection of green onions, so taste a few and see which ones you prefer. Unless otherwise specified, use the entire onion, green and white parts, in my recipes.

To store green onions, practice what we call da-dum-ah, which is to cut off the root ends of the onions, trim any part of the green tops that are brown or discolored, and then wrap the bunch in a paper towel and place in a plastic produce bag, then store in your refrigerator. Stored this way, they will keep well for at least one week. I do not discard the root ends. They are nutritious, fragrant, and have a slight sweetness, so I like to save them to enrich my broths.

JALAPEÑOS

Jalapeños are not native to Korean cooking, but when I moved to Los Angeles, I began to add them to everything I made, including my soon tofu. Now they are a staple in my kitchen when I want to add some heat. Before using, taste a little bit of the raw jalapeño so you can gauge how spicy it really is. Much of the spice comes from the capsaicin in the ribs and seeds of the pepper; if, after tasting, you find the pepper too spicy, remove some of the seeds and ribs to reduce the heat.

MU (KOREAN RADISH)

Mu (also spelled *moo*) are stout, creamy white radishes with a firm, crisp texture that makes them ideal for kimchi, banchan, and soup. They tend to hold quite a bit of water, but how much water will vary depending on the time of the year. Their peak season is late winter, but also look for the delicious radishes from Jeju Island, which often arrive in Korean markets in the spring. When shopping, choose radishes with smooth skins and bright green tops. In Korea, when I was younger, our radishes were often quite fibrous, so we had to peel them before cooking them. Nowadays, many of the radishes sold at the market have thinner skins, especially when they're in season, but feel free to peel the radish if it feels especially thick to you.

NAPA CABBAGE

When shopping for napa cabbage, look for heads that have creamy white stalks. Avoid the cabbage if the stalk is a pale yellow. When you hold the cabbage, it should feel heavy for its size. If a bit of liquid releases when the stalk is squeezed or poked, that's a good sign that it is fresh and will be especially good in kimchi and other dishes.

SOYBEAN SPROUTS

I always have a bag of soybean sprouts in my refrigerator. When shopping, be careful not to confuse these with mung bean sprouts, which are much smaller. Look for soybean sprouts with bright yellow heads and thick white stems. If the stems are thin, the sprouts may be too chewy once cooked. Avoid sprouts that have any bit of green, since that is an indication that they are not fresh. Also note that when raw, the sprouts may have a fishy flavor or aroma; that should disappear once the sprouts are cooked.

Meat and Seafood

I encourage you to source the freshest meat and seafood you can find—it will make a difference in flavor.

SHORT RIB TRIMMINGS

Korean markets package and sell tang yong galbi, which are meaty short ribs intended for use in soup. I almost always pick these up and trim the meat from the bones, saving the bones for broth and the trimmings, with their great balance of flavor and fat content, for my soon tofu and other stew and soup recipes. Because you trim the meat yourself, these bones sell at a fraction of the cost of just the short rib meat. If they are not available in your area, any other fatty cut of beef is a sufficient substitute to flavor your broths and soups.

FISH CAKES

Fish cakes are extremely versatile in Korean cooking and can be added to many banchan and soups. I prefer fish cakes made with snapper or sea bream from either the Wang Foods or Sempio brand. Korean supermarkets carry them in the frozen or refrigerated section. If they're frozen, defrost before using.

SQUID

Fresh whole squid is available at Asian markets, and you can often find squid that has already been cleaned and packaged in the seafood department. Otherwise, source the squid from your local fishmonger and ask them to clean the squid for you.

Pantry Shelf

These items are always in my pantry. Many of these will keep for several months and can be bought in bulk.

CORN SYRUP

While sugar has the purpose of making a dish sweet, corn syrup gives dishes not only sweetness but also shine and color, especially in banchan. Garnishes like toasted sesame seeds, green onions, and seaweed will adhere better to a dish that has a corn syrup glaze. There are many Korean brands of corn syrup; if shopping in a non-Korean market, choose light rather than dark corn syrup since it is more neutral in flavor.

DASHIMA / DRIED SEA KELP

Dashima is a great way to bring umami to foods. I use it in my Anchovy and Dashi Broth (page 48), and I also like to fry it to use in bibimbap or eat it as a snack. Dashima is sold in large sheets at Asian supermarkets. I look for thicker pieces with a beautiful dark green color.

DOENJANG / FERMENTED SOYBEAN PASTE

Doenjang, made of fermented soybeans, is salty, warming, and earthy. Different brands offer different forms and textures. Over the years, I've tried them all and have found that my favorite is a combination of Wang Foods and Chung Jung One (often abbreviated on the packaging as CJ, like my daughter's name) brands, which I mix in equal proportions. I found that these two, with their slightly different textures, salt levels, and depth of flavor, balance beautifully when combined. Of course, you can use any brand you like for the recipes in this book. Note that some doenjangs are preseasoned for use in soup or as a dip (ssamjang)—you want to avoid those for this book. Instead, double-check the label to make sure it simply states "fermented soybean paste." Once you've opened the doenjang, store it in the refrigerator, where it will keep for several months.

DRIED ANCHOVIES

Dried anchovies come in all sizes, and the size you need depends on what you'll be making. I buy the larger-sized dried anchovies (2½ to 3 inches / 6 to 7.5cm in length) to make broth. And for convenience, the packages often state

that the anchovies are intended to be used in stock. Since they're dried, they will last in your pantry for a very long time.

FISH SAUCE

Fish sauce gives banchan and kimchi an irreplaceable fishy, salty, umami flavor. A little goes a long way, so use it with restraint. My preferred brand is Three Crabs Fish Sauce. Some fish sauce contains gluten, so if you are sensitive to gluten, be sure to check the label before using.

GOCHUGARU

Gochugaru are red pepper flakes made from sun-dried Korean peppers (taeyangcho). There are many varieties available, and if you're not familiar with them, it can be a little difficult to sort through the options. I suggest first checking the expiration date and the ingredients. Older gochugaru tends to be duller in color and taste bitter and harsh. The only ingredient should be dried red peppers, and the flakes should be a natural bright red; avoid brands that include artificial coloring to make the flakes brighter and redder. In my experience, that coloring will soften vegetables, especially in kimchi. Second, packages usually indicate the gochugaru's spice level. I usually default to medium because it is easier to add more spice as needed when cooking. Finally, my go-to brand is Assi, but if it is not available, choose a brand with a good reputation (if you're not familiar with Korean brands, choose one that has multiple product lines at the market).

GOCHUJANG

Gochujang is a fermented chile paste used as a base for many sauces, marinades, and dips. Made of gochugaru, fermented soybeans, sweet rice, and barley malt, it is spicy, savory, and sweet all at the same time. My best advice when looking for gochujang is to buy the best you can afford. Once opened, it will keep for several months in the fridge. My preferred brand is Chung Jung One.

RICE

← (top to bottom): Gochujang, Doenjang / Fermented Soy Bean Paste (page 21), and Gochugaru.

I use short-grain white rice. There are many brands of short-grain white rice at Korean supermarkets. Try a few and see which one you like. If you are a bargain hunter, Korean supermarkets often have sales on bags of rice, and many offer discounts or even free bags when you spend a certain amount on groceries.

RICE CAKES

Rice cakes are delicious additions to soups and noodle dishes, and I always have a package in my refrigerator to make quick meals. If you live near a Korean community, you may be able to find fresh rice cakes made without many preservatives, which I encourage you to seek out. Otherwise, packages of rice cakes can be found in the refrigerated or frozen section of Korean supermarkets and at many other markets—even Trader Joe's has rice cakes now! If you do buy the packaged version, make sure you take the time to soak them according to the directions before using; otherwise, they will crumble and lose their shape when cooked.

RICE COOKING WINE

Rice cooking wine tenderizes meat and neutralizes any overtly gamy, meaty smell. It also brings out the flavors of the other ingredients. There are many types of rice cooking wine; be careful not to confuse rice cooking wine with sweet cooking wine. I use michiu, a Chinese rice cooking wine. Look for brands like Empire or Qian Hu at Asian markets as well as online.

SALT

I am biased, but I always use coarse Korean sea salt. It is just salty enough, and the texture allows me to feel with my fingers the right amount I want to use to season my food. As with other types of salt, Korean sea salt comes in a variety of textures and forms, and everyone has their own favorite. To find yours, experiment with a few and taste how it affects the saltiness of your cooking, especially if you use non-Korean sea salt or fine salts: those may be saltier, and you may need to adjust the amount you use as you cook through the recipes.

SESAME OIL

There are toasted and untoasted sesame oils at supermarkets. For this book, use toasted sesame oil, which is much darker in color than the untoasted oil. I use it in all my cooking but especially as a finish; drizzled right at the end, it will enhance the dish with rich, nutty flavor. My preferred brand is Kadoya. I suggest buying a small bottle and replacing it as needed, since it goes rancid quickly. Store this oil in a cool, dark area away from your stove.

SESAME SEEDS

Sesame seeds are sometimes sold in bulk, but I suggest buying a small package, since you may not use all the seeds in the larger packages before they go stale. Markets sell both untoasted and toasted sesame seeds; I much prefer to buy the untoasted seeds and toast them myself, because the pre-toasted seeds sometimes have a bitter, metallic residue from the manufacturing process. Freshly toasted sesame seeds are also vastly superior in taste.

SOY SAUCE

Buy the best soy sauce you can afford—it will make a difference. Soy sauces vary widely in salt level. My preferred brand is Sempio 501 or 701, available at Korean markets and online; this brand is lighter and less salty than many other brands like Kikkoman. If you do end up using another brand of soy sauce, you may need to adjust the seasoning in my recipes, especially the saltiness, or use the soy sauce more sparingly.

SALTED SHRIMP

Jars of slightly fermented, salted shrimp are available in the refrigerated aisle at Korean and other Asian markets. Look for jars with the plumpest and largest shrimp, since the salt will be less concentrated. Before using, I like to puree the shrimp with a little bit of water, so it blends into sauces more evenly. I also think the appearance of whole salted shrimp may be off-putting to some, so blending can make them more palatable. While you may omit salted shrimp in the recipes that call for it, its absence will be notable.

TOFU

When I was growing up in Korea, tofu was sold in carts by individual vendors. The tofu market has come a long way since then! In the United States, tofu is now widely available in the refrigerated section in markets big and small. Tofu is categorized by its texture, and what determines the tofu's texture is its water content: the more water that is pressed out, the firmer the tofu will be.

Generally, which type of tofu to use depends on what you plan to make with it, as well as your own personal preferences. Soon tofu chigae uses soon tofu, or extra-soft tofu. Very little water is pressed out of soon tofu, resulting in a pillowy, soft consistency that is excellent in stews. My favorite brand for soon tofu is Pulmuone, which is commonly available at Korean markets and many Asian markets. The House Foods brand of extra-soft tofu is also very good.

A few of my recipes involve stir-frying or pan-frying tofu. For those recipes, choose a medium or firm tofu, which is dense and sturdy and will not fall apart as you cook it. House Foods also makes very good medium and firm tofu.

No matter the type of tofu, it is best used immediately. If you do have leftovers, discard the liquid from the container and add enough water to cover the remaining tofu plus a pinch of salt and a drop or two of white vinegar. Cover and place in the refrigerator, and use as soon as you can.

Equipment

You likely already have much of the cookware and other equipment necessary to make most of the recipes in this book. Still, there are a few items that are useful to have if you don't already have them. For suggestions on where to source many of these pieces, turn to page 238.

PORTABLE BUTANE BURNER

Portable butane burners allow you to cook right at the table. In addition to using a burner to make Korean BBQ with your family and friends, you can also enlist it to keep soups warm during a meal. I always have a few extra canisters of fuel on hand, so I can use the butane burner when needed.

DOLSOT

Dolsots, or stone pots, retain heat perfectly and, most importantly, will create a bottom layer of crisp rice in bibimbap. Dolsots generally are sold in small, medium, and large sizes at Korean markets; other Asian markets carry them, too, though their selection may be more limited. You can also find a great assortment online. My bibimbap recipes direct you to use two large dolsots about 9½ inches / 24cm in diameter. Season these pots before using.

GLOVES AND APRON

Wear gloves and an apron to avoid staining your hands and clothes when making kimchi. Korean markets are great resources since they sell gloves in various sizes and with varying levels of thickness.

GREEN ONION SHREDDER

These shredders have several blades thinly spaced apart to make it easy for you to shred green onions into thin strips. They are available at many Asian markets as well as online. If you don't have a shredder, you can slice the green onions into thin ribbons with a sharp knife instead.

KIMCHI CONTAINERS

Nonreactive food-grade containers and jars with lids in a variety of sizes are a must to store and ferment your kimchi. Glass mason jars are good options, and plastic containers with vacuum lids specifically intended for fermenting kimchi are also available at many Korean markets, home goods shops, and online retailers. You can even ferment kimchi in resealable freezer bags; this is an especially good option if you are short on refrigerator space. Be sure your selected container is completely clean before using it to make kimchi.

KOREAN BBQ GRILL PANS

These pans are essential for any Korean BBQ meal made at home and can be found at Korean supermarkets. Korean grill pans have plenty of surface area for everyone to grill their own meat and vegetables and have a separate drip tray to collect grease. I highly recommend pans made of cast iron for ease and durability; just be sure to season and care for them as you would any other cast-iron cookware.

SESAME SEED GRINDER

Ground toasted sesame seeds are a great way to finish many dishes, and having your own grinder allows you to grind exactly as much as you need, in the texture you prefer. Pre-ground sesame seeds are also not nearly as flavorful as freshly ground. Even if you already have a spice grinder or a coffee grinder, I suggest you pick up a grinder specifically for sesame seeds, because the seeds release strong aromatic oils when ground. Sesame seed grinders are available at Asian markets, restaurant supply stores, and online.

SCISSORS

Good kitchen scissors are one of the most useful tools for cooks. They are perfect for cutting meats and vegetables, while they're cooking in the pot or when serving. Korean supermarkets and restaurant supply stores have many to choose from.

TTUKBAEGI

Made of earthenware, these are the only vessels I use for cooking and serving soon tofu. They retain heat very, very well, so they will keep your soon tofu hot until the very last bite. Most come with their own trivet or tray; if yours does not have one, be sure to place a trivet underneath the ttukbaegi when bringing it to the table. See detailed instructions on sourcing (page 238), seasoning (page 33), care, and use (page 34).

Soon Tofu Chigae

Soon tofu chigae is a homey, comforting dish. It consists of a bold savory broth filled with delicate soft tofu plus meat, seafood, vegetables, kimchi, or a combination of all of the above. Once you have all the ingredients, the cooking process is relatively straightforward: you build the broth; add the fillings, including the tofu, in multiple stages; then finish with a splash of toasted sesame oil.

The best way to make soon tofu, I believe, is to assemble and cook each serving individually, in its own ttukbaegi. That is how we made it at Beverly Soon Tofu, and it's how I suggest you cook it at home, too. The soon tofu is most robust and vibrant right after it's pulled off the stove, still boiling. In contrast, if you make one large pot and portion the stew from there, you will lose much of its nuance and flavor. In addition, making each serving individually allows everyone at the table to customize their fillings and spice level.

Making each soon tofu to order was a logistical challenge for the restaurant, but no matter how busy we were, I always told my cooks to focus on the ttukbaegi. I encourage you to do the same. Whether you are new to making soon tofu or have made it several times, notice how the flavor and color of the broth transform with the addition of garlic and dadaegi (seasoned red pepper paste). Notice, too, how the flavors develop as each filling is added. And, finally, watch the temperature, being careful to keep it at a boil.

Making soon tofu at home is not difficult but it does require your full attention. This chapter is divided into sections that will guide you through every stage of the soon tofu–making process.

Ttukbaegi and Alternative Cooking Pots

The most common vessel in which to cook and serve soon tofu is a ttukbaegi. This clay pot is ideal because its porous surface retains heat exceptionally well, and it can go from the stove directly to the table. Ttukbaegi are easily found in the houseware or cookware section of Korean and other Asian markets. They're also available online.

SIZING

Ttukbaegi come in a variety of sizes, and you may see a number between 1 and 4 printed on the box or shelf label. I use the No. 3 size, which is about 24 oz / 680g and the perfect size for an individual serving.

SEASONING

Ttukbaegi are very durable, and if properly cared for, will last a very long time. Seasoning them with water and salt before the first use is an important part of that care. Doing so will help remove any impurities that may have remained from the manufacturing process, and the salt will fill in the porous surface, strengthening and protecting it from cracks.

TO SEASON WITH WATER AND SALT

Fill a basin with cold or room-temperature water. Place the ttukbaegi on the stove over medium heat. Add 1 tablespoon of salt and enough water to fill the ttukbaegi about three-quarters full. Bring to a boil, then immediately remove the ttukbaegi from the heat, discard the boiling water, and submerge in the basin. Soak the ttukbaegi for a few hours or overnight. The longer the soak, the stronger the ttukbaegi will be. Remove the ttukbaegi and dry completely. It is now ready to use.

TO SEASON WITH RICE WATER AND SALT

In my experience seasoning thousands of ttukbaegi for the restaurant, this method results in a more durable and longer-lasting ttukbaegi, though it does require an extra step. To begin, rinse the rice as you normally would before cooking it, and instead of discarding the starchy rice water, strain it into the ttukbaegi along with 1 tablespoon of salt. Proceed with the remaining steps as in the method above.

HANDLING A HOT TTUKBAEGI

You can purchase metal tongs specifically designed to pick up and move hot ttukbaegi. These tongs resemble pliers with a clamp at its head and can be found in the cookware aisle of Korean and other Asian markets as well as online. If you don't have these tongs, use oven mitts or pot holders that can handle very high temperatures.

CARE

Once the ttukbaegi is placed over heat on your stove, don't wait too long before adding broth or other liquid, as the direct heat may cause the pot to crack. After cooking a few times in your seasoned ttukbaegi, you may see white residue on the surface. That is okay! It will disappear over time. To clean the ttukbaegi, just use soap and water.

ALTERNATIVES

If you don't have a ttukbaegi, you can make soon tofu in a clay pot that can be used on the stove and brought to the table. Alternatively, cook the soon tofu in a small heavy-bottomed pot, like a Dutch oven, then carefully transfer the stew to a serving bowl. You will lose some heat in the process, but it will still work.

The Components

Every soon tofu has broth and garlic, and most also have at least some dadaegi (seasoned red pepper paste) for spice.

THE BROTH

Soon tofu starts with beef broth, anchovy and dashi broth, or, in a few cases, water. I use beef broth for most of my soon tofus, and I include two beef broth recipes here. The first is a fast and easy broth using short rib trimmings. If you have a few more hours and would like to make a deeply flavorful broth from scratch using beef bones, just as we used to do over the course of two days at the restaurant, turn to the second recipe (see page 44). It yields more broth than you will need for one recipe, so I suggest freezing the leftovers so you will have some on hand to make more soon tofu or another stew or soup.

And if you prefer not to make your own broth at all, Korean markets carry packaged bone broth that will do very well in a pinch.

DADAEGI AND THE SPICE LEVEL

Dadaegi is a seasoned chile paste that gives the soon tofu broth its distinctive crimson color. Every cook has their own version of it: it is that personal and that important. Mine is the heart and soul of my soon tofu (see page 49). Not every soon tofu includes dadaegi, but when it is used, care must be taken. For its flavor to have the most impact, it must completely dissolve in the broth before the fillings are added. And because its flavor permeates so thoroughly, the soon tofu must be constantly stirred so the dadaegi doesn't burn. If it does, the broth will become bitter.

The dadaegi is also responsible for much of the spice in soon tofu. The default spice level for most of my soon tofu is medium, but my recipes show you how to adjust the spice level by adjusting the amount of dadaegi you add (see How Spicy? on page 77).

If the soon tofu is *too* spicy, add more tofu or broth (or both), and use less dadaegi the next time you make a bowl.

GARLIC

Every bowl of soon tofu contains at least one teaspoon of garlic, and the soon tofu would not be the same without it. I use garlic every day, so rather than peeling and chopping the cloves each time I use it, I blend a few heads with water and store it in my refrigerator (see page 49). Doing this not only makes it very convenient for cooking but also mellows out the bite of the garlic. If you prefer, you can substitute the blended garlic with an equal amount of minced or pureed garlic.

VEGETARIAN AND VEGAN SOON TOFU

If you're looking for a vegetarian or vegan-friendly soon tofu, many of my recipes can be adjusted accordingly and I have made notes on recipes where this is possible.

The Fillings

After building the base, it's time to add the fillings.

TOFU

Tofu, of course, is the star of soon tofu! While there are many types of tofu available, there is only one type that is best: soon tofu, or extra-soft tofu. Unlike the other types of tofu, very little water is pressed out of soon tofu, resulting in tofu that is very soft and delicate. It will fall apart if handled too aggressively.

My preferred brand of soon tofu is Pulmuone, which sells its soon tofu in tubes. (If organic soybeans are important to you, Pulmuone also makes organic soon tofu. On the basis of flavor alone, however, I still prefer Pulmuone's nonorganic version.)

If you cannot source Pulmuone, I also recommend the House Foods brand of soon tofu. Try different brands to see what you like. Ideally, you will be able to taste the pure, fresh taste of the soybeans. If you can, avoid silken tofu for soon tofu since it does not have the same texture as soon tofu.

MEAT, SEAFOOD, KIMCHI, AND VEGETABLES

The other fillings in soon tofu can include beef, pork, seafood, kimchi, vegetables, or a combination of all of them. These other fillings complement the main ingredient, the tofu.

This chapter includes recipes for ten of my favorite soon tofu, including several that were included on my restaurant's menu from the very beginning: a combination stew with beef, oysters, and clams; a seafood-only stew; and kimchi with beef or pork.

You may notice that my soon tofu are not overloaded with ingredients. That is intentional. I believe less is more: too many ingredients detract from the tofu and lead to an unbalanced stew. To make excellent soon tofu, you just need a good broth, good dadaegi, good tofu, and a few other high-quality ingredients. For that reason, I strongly encourage you to buy the best-quality meat, seafood, and vegetables you can afford.

THE EGG

At Beverly Soon Tofu, the soon tofu always arrived at the table with a raw egg. If the customer wanted, the server, with just one hand, picked up the egg and cracked it right into the bubbling stew. It was very dramatic.

Eggs aren't always served with soon tofu, but I decided to include them after a visit to Korea right before opening my restaurant. On the recommendation of a taxi driver, I went to a soon tofu spot where there was a server whose only job, it seemed to me, was cracking eggs. He had a basketful of eggs, and he was on roller skates. At the exact moment when the soon tofu was served, he skated over with his egg basket, plucked out an egg, and, with one hand, cracked it right into the bowl. I thought that was great fun. I took that idea back with me to LA and taught all my servers how to break an egg with just one hand. (But I did not teach them how to roller skate. I thought the egg part would be entertaining enough.)

I use small eggs, because I think they are the perfect size for the bowl and add just enough richness to the meal. Many people swirl the egg when it drops into the soon tofu, but I suggest patience. If you swirl immediately, the yolk and whites will disperse, making the soup eggy and diluting the broth's flavor. Instead, allow the soon tofu to swallow the egg. As it does, spoon some of the hot liquid over the yolk and whites. Let the egg cook while you enjoy your soon tofu with rice for a few minutes. Then, when the white of the egg is glossy and just set, carefully lift the egg out of the bowl with your spoon and rest it on your rice. Break the egg over the rice and eat it with the soon tofu. This way you will have a delicious egg flavored by the broth and a perfectly balanced soon tofu.

Cooking and Serving

Once you have the broth, dadaegi, garlic, and other fillings prepared, you are ready to make soon tofu. Cooking the soon tofu happens in stages. You build the broth, then add the fillings a little bit at a time, then finish with sesame oil. After each stage, the broth is returned to a boil. This boiling point is very important, because it allows the flavors of the soon tofu to meld and reach their full complexity.

Because each soon tofu is made individually, the soon tofu recipes in this book make a single serving; to make more than one soon tofu, simply repeat the process with another ttukbaegi or clay pot. To make several servings of soon tofu, it would certainly be easier to prepare one large pot of the stew and portion it into smaller bowls from there. However, the flavor is just not as full and nuanced as when each soon tofu is made from scratch, in its own vessel. The soon tofu is at its very best right after it's cooked. When reheated or reboiled, its flavor flattens and its vibrancy is lost. In addition, cooking each clay pot individually allows you to customize each to your guests' preferences. For example, one guest may request a medium-spicy combination soon tofu with beef, clams, and oysters, while another might want a mildly spicy soon tofu with kimchi and pork. As long as you have the ingredients ready to go, each bowl can accommodate the requests of each guest.

The stoves I had at the restaurant were commercial appliances that maintained a constant temperature, so when we put several ttukbaegi on the stove at the same time, they cooked evenly. Home stoves, however, are much more variable. You may already know this about your stove: one burner may not be as hot as another, or when you cook, one area of your pan may heat faster than the other parts of the pan. As a result, you can place two clay pots on the stove at the same time over what seems like the same level of heat, but one may be slower to come to a boil than the other. Stay focused, then, as you make the soon tofu and adjust for these variations. Remember, too, to constantly stir, or the soon tofu may burn, or the fillings may overcook.

If you are new to making soon tofu, you may benefit from practicing with just one pot first to get a sense of the timing and method.

Soon tofu typically is served as part of an array of dishes that includes rice, banchan, kimchi, and one or two meat or seafood options. These dishes are included in The Soon Tofu Table (page 83), and Other Family Favorites (page 155). I suggest you select a few to serve so everyone can share in the meal while the soon tofu are cooking.

A Few Tips

As you make soon tofu, keep the following in mind:

- **Watch the soon tofu like a baby.** When my cooks had soon tofu on the burners, my servers always knew not to bother them. Making soon tofu requires all your focus. I encourage you to be as attentive as my cooks were when you make soon tofu. Be present. Don't daydream. Don't think about your personal problems. Don't think about what you have to do later in the day. Focus just on the soon tofu in the ttukbaegi. Watch it like a baby. You will be rewarded with a delicious meal!

- **Take your time.** The most common mistake when making soon tofu is rushing the process. Good soon tofu takes time. You are looking for the dadaegi to fully dissolve into the broth and for the soon tofu to reach a strong rolling boil before serving. In total, most of my soon tofu take 10 to 15 minutes to cook.

- **Boiling is critical.** Over the years, I have found that the flavors in my soon tofu come together and take on an extra dimension of flavor once the soon tofu is above the boiling point. At the restaurant, I had a custom stove that could reach extremely high temperatures, and the ttukbaegi were literally surrounded by flames as they cooked! Home stoves don't reach quite the same temperature as restaurant stoves, but if you keep the soon tofu at a constant boil, you can achieve similar results in your kitchen. And note that when you bring the soon tofu to a boil the final time before serving, the perimeter of the soon tofu may reach a boil before its center. If this happens, resist the temptation to turn off the heat. Instead, continue to cook and wait until the entire soon tofu, including its very center, is at a vigorous boil before serving.

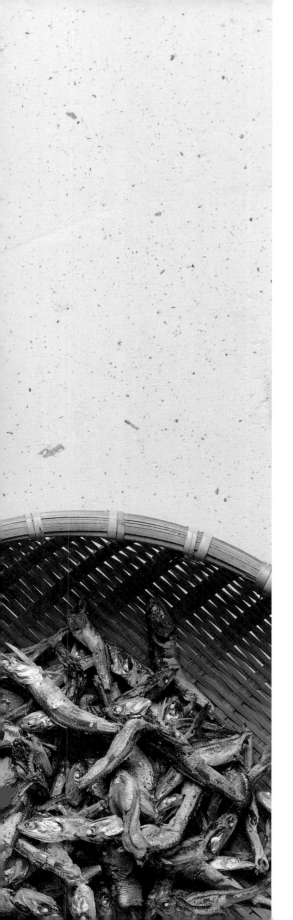

Broths and Bases

A flavorful broth, a vibrant red pepper paste, plus plenty of garlic: these are the building blocks for my soon tofu. Indeed, most of my soon tofu recipes begin by layering these three components to create a complex foundation for the stew. Once you prepare these components, you are well on your way to making a delicious chigae.

All these recipes keep well, so if you plan to make soon tofu often, I suggest doubling them and storing the leftovers in your freezer to save you time in the future. They can also be used in other recipes throughout the book.

GEUPSOK GOGI GUKMUL

급속고기국물

Fast Beef Broth

Makes about 2 qt / 1.9L

This beef broth takes less than an hour to make from start to finish, and all you need are some short rib trimmings (or any other fatty cut of beef) and plenty of water. Though it is lighter and less nuanced than broth made from boiling beef bones for several hours (see page 44) it is delicious nonetheless. It's also faster to make and doesn't require you to source any bones.

2   cups (about 1 lb / 450g) short rib trimmings (see page 20)

1 Place a large pot over high heat, add 10 cups / 2.4L water, and bring to a boil. While the water comes to a boil, place the beef in a large bowl and cover with cold tap water to release any excess blood.

2 Once the water reaches a boil, use tongs to transfer the beef from its bowl to the pot, discard the soaking water. Boil on high heat for 20 to 25 minutes. Using a fine-mesh strainer or a colander, strain the broth, reserving the solids. The broth can be used immediately or stored; first cool completely, then pour into airtight containers and refrigerate for up to 3 days or freeze for up to 1 month. The cooked beef can be repurposed for another use (see Spinoff) or discarded.

GLUTEN-FREE

SPINOFF

If you don't want to discard the cooked beef, try marinating it for 15 to 20 minutes with 2 tablespoons Gahreun Mahneul / Blended Garlic (page 49), 1 tablespoon fish sauce, 1 teaspoon toasted sesame oil, 2 teaspoons sea salt, and ½ teaspoon ground black pepper. Then add the beef to a soup and enjoy it with a hot bowl of rice for a quick meal.

At Beverly Soon tofu, we always made our broth from scratch and cooked it over a two-day period. We used a combination of knee and leg bones and rich, meaty short rib bones. At any given time, we had 200 lb / 91kg of these bones stacked in huge stockpots filled with water rolling at a full boil. Being located in Koreatown was a big advantage, since I was able to make great connections with local butchers who supplied other Korean restaurants and were well stocked with the type of bones needed to make our broth.

Making a similar broth at home is possible, but it does present unique challenges. First, time: The bones need to be soaked, cleaned, and simmered over the course of several hours, so the broth will take the better part of a day to make. Second, space: You will need enough room on your stove for two large stockpots as well as space in your refrigerator or freezer to store what you don't immediately use. For those reasons, I generally recommend making the quicker and less labor-intensive Fast Beef Broth (page 42) or buying prepackaged bone broth at Korean markets. But if you do have the time, space, and interest, making bone broth from scratch is very rewarding. For your efforts, you will end up with a deeply satisfying, beefy broth that will give your soon tofu an unmatched depth of flavor.

To start, you will need a minimum of 5 lb / 2.3kg of knee and leg bones and 5 lb / 2.3kg of short rib bones. Knee and leg bones can be found at many supermarkets, including Asian markets. Short rib bones may be a little trickier to find. If you are unable to source just the bones from your local market or butcher, you can pick up bone-in short ribs and separate the bones yourself, saving the meat for a meal. Alternatively, whenever you have bone-in short ribs, separate the meat from the bones and freeze the raw bones in a resealable plastic bag, until you have enough to make this broth. Given their rich flavor, I do think it is worth the effort to seek out the short rib bones, but if you must, you can substitute them with an equal amount of knee and leg bones.

While the broth simmers, you will need to constantly skim the fat and impurities as they rise to the surface, just as we did at the restaurant. This may seem like a long time to watch over the pots, but it is the key to great beef broth: the more impurities removed, the better the broth. Spending the time to make this broth is certainly a labor of love, but not only will the results be delicious, you will also end up with enough broth to make soon tofu and other soups and stews for your family. Leftovers should be cooled, then poured into airtight containers. It can be refrigerated for up to one week or frozen for up to one month.

5   to 6 lb / 2.3 to 2.7kg short rib bones
5   to 6 lb / 2.3 to 2.7kg knee and leg bones

1 Place the short rib bones in one or more large bowls and the knee/leg bones in separate large bowls. Add enough water to cover all the bones and soak them for 2 hours in the fridge. Discard the water and cover the bones again in water and soak for another 2 hours in the fridge.

2 After 4 hours of soaking, drain and rinse the bones until the water runs clear.

3 Fill two 12- or 16-qt / 11- or 15L stockpots about halfway full with water and bring to a boil over high heat. Drop the short rib bones in one pot and the knee/leg bones in the other. The water should just cover the bones; if it doesn't, add a few more cups until it does. The short rib bones need less time than the knee and leg bones to release their flavor, and I use just enough water to slightly concentrate that flavor before combining it with the broth produced by the knee and leg bones. The two types of bones also release different types of impurities, which are easier to remove if the bones are cooked separately.

CONTINUED

4 Cover and boil for 10 to 15 minutes, then uncover and use a ladle or spoon to remove any foam that has risen to the top. Drain and rinse each bone with cold tap water to remove any residual impurities, taking care to rinse each side and between the meat and the bone.

5 Place the bones back into their separate pots. Pour 5 qt / 4.7L water into the pot with the short rib bones and 7½ qt / 7.1L water into the pot with the knee and leg bones, adding more water only if necessary to cover the bones entirely. Over high heat, boil, uncovered, for 2½ hours or until the broth of the short rib bones turns cloudy and the meat and cartilage are almost separated from the bones. Every 30 minutes, check on both pots and, using a ladle or spoon, skim any foam and fat that rise to the surface. Check on the water level, too: as the pots boil, add as much water as necessary to keep the bones just covered.

6 After 2½ hours, use tongs to remove the short rib bones from the pot. Remove the meat and cartilage and reserve them for another use (the meat from the bones is delicious with some rice; see Spinoff, opposite). Transfer the short rib bones and broth to the pot with the knee/leg bones.

7 Continue boiling, uncovered, for another 1½ hours, still adding water if necessary to cover the bones. Place a mesh strainer over a container and strain the broth. You should have about 2 qt / 1.9L broth. Set aside.

8 Discard the short rib bones and place the knee and leg bones back into the pot and set it over high heat. Pour another 5 qt / 4.7L water into the pot, adding additional water as necessary to cover the bones entirely. Boil

for another 2 hours, still skimming all fat and impurities that rise to the top and adding water as necessary to keep the bones submerged. By the end of 2 hours, your broth should be cloudy and the light cream color of skim milk. If it is not, pour just enough water into the pot to cover the bones and boil a while longer. If you don't remove most of the impurities, the broth will be tinged yellow rather than white. It will still be fine to use, but its flavor may be a little muddled.

9 Strain the broth through a mesh strainer into a large bowl or other container. Discard

the bones. You should end up with about another 2 qt / 1.9L broth. Pour it back into the pot and add the reserved 2 qt/ 1.9L broth from the previous batch. Boil them together for 20 minutes, then turn off the heat.

10 The broth can be used as soon as it's ready, but I recommend refrigerating the broth overnight so the fat solidifies at the top. In the morning, skim the fat with a spoon and discard, and you will have a broth that has the clean flavor of pure beef.

GLUTEN-FREE

SPINOFF

You can marinate the meat from the short ribs and add it to your broth for a delicious meal. To do so, separate the meat from the cartilage. For every 1 cup / 225g meat, add 1 tablespoon Gahreun Mahneul / Blended Garlic (page 49), 1 teaspoon sea salt, 1 teaspoon fish sauce, 2 chopped green onions, and ½ teaspoon ground black pepper. Mix everything together and marinate the meat for 10 to 15 minutes. Add the meat mixture to a bowl of the broth and eat with rice and kimchi.

MYEOLCHI DASHIMA GUKMUL
멸치다시마국물

Anchovy and Dashi Broth

Makes about 3 qt / 2.8L

This broth is a classic in Korean cooking. It's lighter than, say, beef broth, making it a great base for a range of soups and stews. You can use it in my Doenjang Soon Tofu / Soybean Paste Soon Tofu (page 75) and soybean soups (see pages 225, 227, and 232). Packages of dried anchovies are easily found at Asian markets; when shopping, look for those marked specifically for use as a soup (or dashi) base. If in doubt, choose the larger-sized anchovies, 2½ to 3 inches / 6.5 to 7.5cm long, with bodies tinged yellow and a black stripe running down the back. It is important to take the time to remove the intestines of the anchovies; otherwise, the broth will darken and taste bitter.

- 1 cup / 60g dried anchovies
- 1 cup (1 oz / 30g) dashima / dried sea kelp
- ½ lb / 225g mu (Korean radish), unpeeled and quartered (1 small or medium radish)
- ½ lb / 225g yellow onion, unpeeled, washed, and quartered (1 medium onion)
- ½ cup / 30g katsuobushi (dried bonito flakes)
- ½ cup / 120ml rice cooking wine (or soju)

1 Clean an anchovy by gently holding the body with one hand and twisting the head with the other. The head should come off easily, with the innards attached; set aside the head and discard the innards. If some innards remain even after removing the head, split the body and finish gutting the fish. Repeat with the remaining anchovies.

2 Place a small skillet over medium heat. Add the anchovies to the dry pan and toast until fragrant, 1 to 2 minutes, flipping the anchovies about halfway through.

3 Place a large stockpot over high heat, add 5 qt / 4.7L water, and bring to a boil. Add the anchovies, reserved anchovy heads, dashima, radish, and onion to the water. Continue boiling for 30 minutes, then add the katsuobushi and cooking wine. Reduce the heat to medium and boil for 5 minutes more, until the broth is a light, clear yellow color.

4 Turn off the heat and let cool, then strain through a colander. Discard the solids and use the broth immediately or store in airtight containers in the refrigerator for up to 1 week. Alternatively, pour the cooled broth into gallon-sized resealable plastic bags and lay them flat in the freezer to save space. Frozen, the broth will last up to 1 month.

GLUTEN-FREE

Seasoned Red Pepper Paste

Makes about ½ cup / 160g

Every Korean restaurant has its own signature dadaegi, and this is mine. I have treasured this recipe for the last thirty-five years; it is the heart and soul of every soon tofu soup I make, the base that enlivens the stew with a medley of spiciness, saltiness, sweetness, and richness. It has many uses beyond soon tofu, too. Use it to build flavor in my Gochujang Chigae / Red Pepper Paste Stew with Tofu (page 224) or the Spicy Squid Soup (page 231). It is very simple to make, but it does require two days to develop its flavor. Because it is so versatile and stores so well, I suggest making plenty. Back when I ran my restaurant, I made gallons and gallons. In fact, the longer it sits, the deeper and more complex the flavors become.

- ¼ cup / 45g coarse gochugaru
- ¼ cup / 30g fine gochugaru
- ¼ cup / 60ml soy sauce
- 1 teaspoon sea salt
- 1 teaspoon fish sauce
- 1 teaspoon granulated sugar

In a medium bowl, combine ¼ cup / 60ml water with the coarse and fine gochugaru, soy sauce, salt, fish sauce, and sugar. Mix until the sugar has dissolved and the gochugaru are well incorporated. Place the mixture in a glass container and cover. Leave at room temperature for 1 day, then place in the refrigerator. It's ready to use the next morning. Store for up to 1 month in the fridge.

▶▶▶ **To make a vegetarian or vegan version,** omit the fish sauce and increase the salt to 1½ teaspoons. Mix and store as instructed.

Blended Garlic

Makes 1½ to 2 cups / 375 to 500g

Garlic is in almost everything I make. As a time-saving measure, rather than peeling and mincing every time I needed it, I decided to try blending heads of garlic with water and seeing if it lost its flavor—and it didn't! In fact, I found that blended garlic actually mellowed and its flavor became more balanced, even after a week or two in the fridge. Add this garlic to all your dishes but do be careful when adding it to hot oil: the water in the mixture may cause the oil to spatter. Once made, it will keep in the refrigerator for up to ten days. Discard the garlic when its color turns from pale yellow to brown.

- 2 cups / 300g whole peeled garlic cloves

1 Slice off the root ends of the garlic cloves and discard. If any of the cloves have sprouted, slice the clove in half lengthwise and remove and discard the green germ.

2 Place the garlic in a blender and add ¾ cup / 175ml water. Blend until smooth or until it has the consistency of applesauce, adding up to ¼ cup / 60ml more water if necessary to reach that consistency. It's now ready to use. Store any leftovers in an airtight container in the refrigerator.

VEGETARIAN, VEGAN, GLUTEN-FREE

Freshly Toasted Sesame Seeds

Make as much as you'd like

There is a world of difference between the bright, richly nutty flavor of freshly toasted sesame seeds and the muted, duller taste of pre-toasted seeds. For that reason, I always buy untoasted sesame seeds and toast them myself, washing the seeds first to remove the metallic, bitter-tasting residue that often remains from the manufacturing process. If you are new to toasting sesame seeds, I suggest working with just a few handfuls at a time to avoid burning them. The more you practice and gain a sense of the timing, the more you can toast.

Untoasted white sesame seeds

1 Place the sesame seeds in a fine-mesh strainer and wash several times under running water. Drain them as best you can.

2 Place a dry skillet or wok over high heat. Once the pan is hot, add the seeds and stir. It is critical to keep stirring so the seeds toast evenly and don't burn. As you stir, listen: once you hear the seeds begin to crackle, reduce the heat to low. Keep stirring.

3 As the seeds toast, the nutty aroma alone will tell you when they're ready. Another sign is the color changing from pale white to golden brown. Depending on the quantity, it may take anywhere from just a few minutes to several minutes for the seeds to toast.

4 Immediately transfer the seeds to a large bowl or plate. Cool completely, then store in small airtight containers for up to 1 month in the pantry and up to 3 months in the fridge.

VEGETARIAN, VEGAN, GLUTEN-FREE

Soon Tofu Chigae

Of the many, many soon tofu I have made over the last three decades, these ten are my favorites. Note that each recipe serves one person. To serve more than one, simply repeat the process with another ttukbaegi. To that end, each recipe also includes a box that shows how much of each ingredient is needed to serve a small party of four. Each serving of soon tofu should still be made in its own single-serving clay pot, but the guide, I hope, will be a convenient reference for you as you shop for the ingredients.

Whichever soon tofu you make, be sure to serve it with plenty of steamed rice, a few banchan (see page 87) and kimchi (see page 123) for the table, and, optionally, a large platter or two (see page 175) to share, too.

섞어 순두부

Combination Soon Tofu

Serves 1

When I opened Beverly Soon Tofu in 1986, I had four soon tofu options on the menu. This combination of beef, oysters, and clams was one of them. I created this recipe for a few reasons. I believed customers would want a little bit of everything in their soon tofu stew, and by having a little bit of everything, they would feel that the soon tofu was a good value, well worth their time and money. Plus, all these ingredients just taste delicious together, especially if you use flavorful Manila clams. I intentionally omit shrimp , as I find the flavor of shrimp to be overpowering here. While the recipe instructs you to make the soon tofu as four individual servings, you'll be marinating the short rib trimmings in one large batch.

For 1 individual soon tofu

- 1 cup / 240ml homemade beef broth (page 42 or 44) or store-bought
- 2 tablespoons Dadaegi / Seasoned Red Pepper Paste (page 49), or to taste (see How Spicy? on page 77)
- 1 teaspoon Gahreun Mahneul / Blended Garlic (page 49)
- ¼ cup / 55g marinated short rib trimmings
- 3 baby clams, preferably Manila
- 3 to 4 small shucked oysters
- 1 (11-oz / 312g) package extra-soft tofu
  Toasted sesame oil, for finishing
  Handful of green onions, green and white parts, chopped, for garnish
- 1 small egg

TO MAKE THE SOON TOFU

1 Place a clay pot over high heat. Add ½ cup / 120ml of the beef broth, the dadaegi, garlic, and marinated trimmings and stir. Bring to a boil and cook until the beef is cooked all the way through and no longer pink, about 5 minutes.

2 Add the clams and oysters and boil until the clams open and the oysters are fully cooked, 4 to 6 minutes (discard any clams that do not open). Add ½ package tofu and the remaining ½ cup / 120ml beef broth. Use a spoon to divide the tofu into smaller pieces, then stir to distribute the pieces, doing so gently to avoid breaking up the tofu any further. Be sure to stir the bottom of the pot, too, to prevent burning. Skim any fat or other impurities with your spoon as they rise to the surface.

CONTINUED

3 Stop stirring and bring the soon tofu back to a boil. Add another ¼ package of tofu to the pot, dividing it into smaller pieces with your spoon, and stir gently again. Bring the pot to a boil, then add the remaining ¼ package of tofu and stir.

4 Continue to cook for 10 to 15 minutes, or until the center of the soon tofu is at a rapid boil. Finish with a splash of sesame oil and the green onions. Crack the egg into the pot. Allow the egg to cook, undisturbed, until the whites are firm and the yolk is as done as you'd like.

5 Serve boiling hot on a trivet at the table along with the banchan, kimchi, and any shared platter you may have prepared.

Marinated Short Rib Trimmings

Makes enough for 4 servings of soon tofu

- 1 **cup (about ½ lb / 225g) short rib trimmings, sliced into bite-sized pieces**
- ½ **teaspoon Gahreun Mahneul / Blended Garlic (page 49)**
- ½ **teaspoon toasted sesame oil**
- ½ **teaspoon Sea salt**

TO MARINATE THE TRIMMINGS: In a medium bowl, combine the short rib trimmings, sesame oil, garlic, and salt and marinate for 20 to 30 minutes.

- **4** cups / 950ml homemade beef broth (page 42 or 44) or store-bought
- **8** tablespoons / 160g Dadaegi / Seasoned Red Pepper Paste (page 49), or to taste (see How Spicy? on page 77)
- **4** teaspoons Gahreun Mahneul / Blended Garlic
- **1** cup / 225g marinated short rib trimmings
- **12** baby clams, preferably Manila
- **12** to 16 small shucked oysters
- **4** (11-ounce / 312g) packages extra-soft tofu
  Toasted sesame oil, for finishing
- **½** bunch green onions, green and white parts, chopped, for finishing
- **4** small eggs

BEOSEOT SOGOGI SOON TOFU

버섯 소고기 순두부

Mushroom and Beef Soon Tofu

Serves 1

People seem to either love mushrooms or hate them. This soon tofu is for the mushroom lovers (and based on the popularity of this dish at my restaurant, there are many mushroom lovers in Los Angeles!). The base for this soon tofu is beef broth, and there are short rib trimmings here, too. Both complement the meaty flavor of the mushrooms perfectly. While the recipe instructs you to make the soon tofu as four individual servings, you'll be marinating the short rib trimmings in one large batch.

For 1 individual soon tofu

- 1 cup / 240ml homemade beef broth (page 42 or 44) or store-bought
- ½ cup / 115g marinated short rib trimmings
- 2 tablespoons Dadaegi / Seasoned Red Pepper Paste (page 49), or to taste (see How Spicy? on page 77)
- 1 teaspoon Gahreun Mahneul / Blended Garlic (page 49)
- ½ cup / 64g sliced button mushrooms
- 1 (11-oz / 312g) package extra-soft tofu Toasted sesame oil, for finishing Handful of green onions, green and white parts, chopped, for garnish
- 1 small egg

TO MAKE THE SOON TOFU

1 Place a clay pot over high heat. Add the ½ cup / 120ml of the beef broth, marinated trimmings, the dadaegi, garlic, and mushrooms and stir. Cook until the beef is cooked all the way through and no longer pink, the dadaegi has fully dissolved, turning the broth bright red, and the broth is at a full boil, about 5 minutes.

2 Add ½ package tofu and the remaining ½ cup / 120ml beef broth. Use a spoon to divide the tofu into smaller pieces, then stir to distribute the pieces, doing so gently to avoid breaking up the tofu any further. Be sure to stir the bottom of the pot, too, to prevent burning, and skim any fat or other impurities as they rise to the surface.

3 Stop stirring and bring the soon tofu back to a boil. Add ¼ package of tofu to the pot, dividing it into smaller pieces with your spoon, and stir gently again. Bring the pot to a boil, then add the remaining ¼ package of tofu to the pot and stir.

4 Continue to cook until the center of the soon tofu is at a rapid boil, about 10 minutes. Finish with a splash of sesame oil and the green onions. Crack the egg into the pot. Allow the egg to cook, undisturbed, until the whites are firm and the yolk is as done as you'd like.

5 Serve boiling hot on a trivet at the table along with the banchan, kimchi, and any shared platter you may have prepared.

Marinated Short Rib Trimmings

Makes enough for 4 servings of soon tofu

- 2 cups (about 1 lb / 450g) short rib trimmings, sliced into bite-sized pieces
- 1 teaspoon Gahreun Mahneul / Blended Garlic (page 49)
- 1 teaspoon toasted sesame oil
- 1 teaspoon Sea salt

TO MARINATE THE TRIMMINGS: In a medium bowl, combine the short rib trimmings, sesame oil, garlic, and salt and marinate for 20 to 30 minutes.

QUICK REFERENCE:
QUANTITIES FOR 4 CLAY POTS

- 4 cups / 950ml homemade beef broth (page 42 or 44) or store-bought
- 2 cups / 450g marinated short rib trimmings (above)
- 8 tablespoons / 160g Dadaegi / Seasoned Red Pepper Paste (page 49), or to taste (see How Spicy? on page 77)
- 4 teaspoons Gahreun Mahneul / Blended Garlic (page 49)
- 2 cups / 450g sliced button mushrooms
- 4 (11-oz / 312g) packages extra-soft tofu
  Toasted sesame oil, for finishing
- ½ bunch green onions, green and white parts, chopped, for garnish
- 4 small eggs

GOGI KIMCHI SOON TOFU

고기 김치 순두부

Beef or Pork Kimchi Soon Tofu

Serves 1

When kimchi overripens and is overly sour, put it to good use in this soon tofu. Here its sourness is an asset since it will stand up well against the other strong flavors of the stew. (I don't suggest using ripe kimchi, since ripe kimchi's most prized characteristics—its sweetness and crunch—will be lost in the stew.) Either beef or pork is delicious here; whichever you choose, select pieces that still have a bit of fat on them, since the fat will help the kimchi's rich flavor shine through. That flavor in turn will be absorbed by the tofu, and every bite will just about melt in your mouth. If you would like less heat, start with 1 teaspoon Dadaegi / Seasoned Red Pepper Paste per serving. If you would like more heat, add 2 tablespoons Dadaegi / Seasoned Red Pepper Paste per serving. For an extra spicy stew, you can also add jalapeño slices. While the recipe instructs you to make the soon tofu as four individual servings, you'll be marinating the meat in one large batch.

For 1 individual soon tofu

- 1 cup / 240ml homemade beef broth (page 42 or 44) or store-bought
- ½ cup / 115g marinated meat
- ¼ cup / 100g kimchi, preferably overripened, chopped
- 4½ teaspoons Dadaegi / Seasoned Red Pepper Paste (page 49), or to taste
- 1 teaspoon Gahreun Mahneul / Blended Garlic (page 49)
- 1 (11-oz / 312g) package extra-soft tofu
  Toasted sesame oil, for finishing
  Handful of green onions, green and white parts, chopped, for garnish
- 1 small egg

TO MAKE THE SOON TOFU

1 Place a clay pot over high heat. Add ½ cup / 120ml of the beef broth, the marinated meat, kimchi, dadaegi, and garlic. Cook until the meat is cooked all the way through, the dadaegi has fully dissolved (the broth should turn a bright red), and the broth is at a full boil, about 5 minutes.

2 Add ½ package of tofu to the pot. Use a spoon to divide the tofu into smaller pieces, then stir to distribute the pieces, doing so gently to avoid breaking up the tofu any further. Be sure to stir the bottom of the pot, too, to prevent burning, and skim any fat or other impurities as they rise to the surface. Add the remaining ½ cup / 120ml beef broth.

3 Stop stirring and bring the soon tofu back to a boil. Add ¼ package of tofu to the pot, dividing it into smaller pieces with your spoon, and stir gently again. Bring the pot to a boil, then add the remaining ¼ package of tofu to the pot and stir.

4 Cook until the center of the soon tofu is at a rapid boil, about 10 minutes. Finish with a splash of sesame oil and the green onions. Crack the egg into the pot. Allow the egg to cook, undisturbed, until the whites are firm and the yolk is as done as you'd like.

5 Serve boiling hot on a trivet at the table along with the banchan, kimchi, and any shared platter you may have prepared.

Marinated Meat

Makes enough for 4 servings of soon tofu

- 2 cups (about 1 lb / 450g) short rib trimmings or pork neck or pork belly, sliced into bite-sized pieces
- 1 teaspoon Gahreun Mahneul / Blended Garlic (page 49)
- 1 teaspoon toasted sesame oil
- 1 teaspoon Sea salt

TO MARINATE THE MEAT: In a medium bowl, combine the meat, garlic, sesame oil, and salt and marinate for 20 to 30 minutes.

QUICK REFERENCE:
QUANTITIES FOR 4 CLAY POTS

- 4 cups / 950ml homemade beef broth (page 42 or 44) or store-bought
- 6 tablespoons / 120g Dadaegi / Seasoned Red Pepper Paste (page 49), or to taste (see headnote)
- 4 teaspoons Gahreun Mahneul / Blended Garlic (page 49)
- 1 cup / 225g marinated meat (above)
- 1 cup / 400g kimchi, preferably overripened, chopped
- 4 (11-oz / 312g) packages extra-soft tofu
  Toasted sesame oil, for finishing
- ½ bunch green onions, green and white parts, chopped, for garnish
- 4 small eggs

HAEMUL SOON TOFU

해물 순두부

Seafood Soon Tofu

Serves 1

When I was a child in Korea, fresh seafood was always very expensive and thus was considered a luxury to have. But here in the United States now, fresh high-quality seafood is not as costly. This soon tofu came together because I love how seafood complements the spice in soon tofu. I also welcomed the opportunity to offer my customers a deluxe soon tofu that was still affordable. Because the shellfish are such an important part of this soon tofu, choose the best you can afford. Manila clams in particular have a great depth of flavor. Black mussels can be used if you are unable to source green mussels.

For 1 individual soon tofu

- 1 cup / 240ml homemade beef broth (page 42 or 44) or store-bought
- 2 tablespoons Dadaegi / Seasoned Red Pepper Paste (page 49), or to taste (see How Spicy? on page 77)
- 1 teaspoon Gahreun Mahneul / Blended Garlic (page 49)
- 2 medium green mussels, cleaned
- 2 small shucked oysters
- 2 (61/70-size) shrimp (meaning 61 to 70 are equal to a pound), heads and shells on
- 2 baby clams, preferably Manila
- 1 (11-oz / 312g) package extra-soft tofu Toasted sesame oil, for finishing Handful of green onions, green and white parts, chopped, for garnish
- 1 small egg

TO MAKE THE SOON TOFU

1 Place a clay pot over high heat. Add ½ cup / 120ml of the beef broth, the dadaegi, and garlic and stir. Cook for about 5 minutes, until the broth is at a full boil and the dadaegi has fully dissolved, turning the broth bright red.

2 Add the mussels, oysters, shrimp, and clams to the pot and boil until the shrimp are firm and opaque and the mussels and clams have opened (discard any mussel or clam that does not open).

3 Add ½ package of tofu and the remaining ½ cup / 120ml beef broth. Use a spoon to divide the tofu into smaller pieces, then stir to distribute the pieces, doing so gently to avoid breaking up the tofu any further. Be sure to stir the bottom of the pot, too, to prevent burning. Use your spoon to skim any fat or other impurities as they rise to the surface.

4 Stop stirring and bring the soon tofu back to a boil. Add another ¼ package of tofu to the pot, dividing it into smaller pieces with your spoon, and stir gently again. Bring the pot to a boil, then add the remaining ¼ package of tofu to the pot and stir.

5 Cook until the center of the soon tofu is at a rapid boil, about 10 minutes. Finish with a splash of sesame oil and the green onions. Crack the egg into the pot. Allow the egg to cook, undisturbed, until the whites are firm and the yolk is as done as you'd like.

6 Serve boiling hot on a trivet at the table along with the banchan, kimchi, and any shared platter you may have prepared.

QUICK REFERENCE:
QUANTITIES FOR 4 CLAY POTS

- 4 cups / 950ml homemade beef broth (page 42 or 44) or store-bought
- 8 tablespoons / 160g Dadaegi / Seasoned Red Pepper Paste (page 49), or to taste (see How Spicy? on page 77)
- 4 teaspoons Gahreun Mahneul / Blended Garlic (page 49)
- 8 medium green mussels, cleaned
- 8 small shucked oysters
- 8 (61/70-size) shrimp (meaning 61 to 70 are equal to a pound), heads and shells on
- 8 baby clams, preferably Manila
- 4 (11-oz / 312g) packages extra-soft tofu
  Toasted sesame oil, for finishing
- ½ bunch green onions, green and white parts, chopped, for garnish
- 4 small eggs

AHL SOON TOFU

알 순두부

Roe Soon Tofu

Serves 1

While roe is a common ingredient in Korean cooking, especially in stews, it's not a traditional filling for soon tofu. But many of my customers loved the taste of roe, so I was inspired to try adding it to my soon tofu. I experimented with different types of roe before deciding to use plump, briny cod roe; when added to a soon tofu, it takes on a savory, almost roasted flavor that pairs nicely with the tofu. And in contrast to smaller roe varieties, it's less likely to become tough and chewy when boiled. Use frozen cod roe, which you'll find at Asian grocers; it can be fragile, so salting it for a few hours before cooking will help the roe keep its shape and prevent it from disintegrating in the hot broth. If you can't find frozen cod roe, you can use frozen unsalted pollock roe instead. I don't recommend using fresh cod roe, since it's generally more difficult to source, will fall apart in the boiling broth, and is often preseasoned with salt and other spices that do not go well with the stew. Finally, use any combination of zucchini, onions, mushrooms, and mu (Korean radish) that you like. If you do include mushrooms, I suggest button, cremini, trumpet, or oyster mushrooms. Avoid shiitake mushrooms, as their flavor is too strong for this dish. While the recipe instructs you to make the soon tofu as four individual servings, you'll be salting the roe in one large batch.

For 1 individual soon tofu

- 1 cup / 240ml homemade beef broth (page 42 or 44) or store-bought, plus more as needed
- 2 tablespoons Dadaegi / Seasoned Red Pepper Paste (page 49), or to taste (see How Spicy? on page 77)
- 1 teaspoon Gahreun Mahneul / Blended Garlic (page 49)
- ½ cup / 60g sliced (about 1 inch / 2.5cm) zucchini, onions, mushrooms, and Korean radishes
- ½ cup / 155g frozen salted cod roe
- 1 (11-oz / 312g) package extra-soft tofu
  Toasted sesame oil, for finishing
  Handful of green onions, green and white parts, chopped, for garnish
- 1 small egg

TO MAKE THE SOON TOFU

1 Place a clay pot over high heat. Add ½ cup / 120ml of the beef broth, the dadaegi, and garlic and stir. Cook until the broth is at a full boil and the dadaegi has fully dissolved, turning the broth bright red, about 5 minutes.

2 Keeping the heat on high, add the vegetables, salted roe, and remaining ½ cup / 120ml beef broth. Use a spoon to gently stir to distribute the fillings, being careful not to overstir, or the roe will fall apart. Continue to boil until the vegetables are tender and cooked through. As the soon tofu boils, the roe will absorb quite a bit of broth; add up to ¼ cup / 60ml more broth as needed to avoid burning.

3 Add ⅓ package of tofu. Use your spoon to divide the tofu into smaller pieces, then gently stir to distribute the pieces, taking care to avoid breaking up the tofu any further. Be sure to stir the bottom of the pot, too, to prevent burning.

4 Stop stirring and bring the soon tofu back to a boil. Add another ⅓ package of tofu to the pot, dividing it into smaller pieces with your spoon, and stir gently again. Bring the pot to a boil, then add the remaining ⅓ package of tofu to the pot and stir.

5 Cook until the center of the soon tofu is at a rapid boil, about 10 minutes. Finish with a splash of sesame oil and the green onions. Crack the egg into the pot. Allow the egg to cook, undisturbed, until the whites are firm and the yolk is as done as you'd like.

6 Serve boiling hot on a trivet at the table along with the banchan, kimchi, and any shared platter you may have prepared.

Salted Cod Roe

Makes enough for 4 servings of soon tofu

> 2 cups (1 lb / 450g) frozen cod roe
> Sea salt

TO PREPARE THE ROE: Place the roe in a large bowl and thaw overnight in the refrigerator. The next day, rinse with cold tap water and pat dry with a paper towel. Cut into 1-inch / 2.5 cm pieces. Return the roe to the bowl and sprinkle all sides with a few generous pinches of salt. Freeze for at least 2 hours. When you're ready to make the soon tofu, remove the roe from the freezer.

QUICK REFERENCE:
QUANTITIES FOR 4 CLAY POTS

- 4 cups / 950ml homemade beef broth (pages 42 or 44)
- 8 tablespoons / 160 g Dadaegi / Seasoned Red Pepper Paste (page 49), or to taste (see How Spicy? on page 77)
- 4 teaspoons Gahreun Mahneul / Blended Garlic (page 49)
- 2 cups / 240g combination of sliced (about 1 inch / 2.5cm) zucchini, onions, mushrooms, and Korean radishes
- 2 cups / 450g frozen salted cod roe (above)
- 4 (11-oz / 312g) packages extra-soft tofu
  Toasted sesame oil, for finishing
- ½ bunch green onions, green and white parts, chopped, for garnish
- 4 small eggs

Shrimp and Vegetable Soon Tofu

Serves 1

When I was growing up in Korea, shrimp were expensive and difficult to find. Whenever I had a chance to eat them, it was such a treat! Nowadays, fresh shrimp are much more accessible, and I think they're perfect in soon tofu. They add a light brininess to the soup's broth without additional heaviness. They also absorb much of the broth's flavors. Each individual bowl here should have four shrimp, no more, no less, because I have found that three shrimp don't add quite enough seafood flavor to the broth, and five add too much. Four is just right. The vegetables, a combination of zucchini, onion, mushrooms, and Korean radish, all complement the shrimp well; I especially like to use button, cremini, trumpet, or oyster mushrooms here. This soon tofu will satisfy all seafood lovers. It's best served hot, with at least a medium level of heat; the dadaegi really brings out the taste of the shrimp.

For 1 individual soon tofu

- 1 cup / 240ml homemade beef broth (page 42 or 44) or store-bought
- 2 tablespoons Dadaegi / Seasoned Red Pepper Paste (page 49), or to taste (see How Spicy? on page 77)
- 1 teaspoon Gahreun Mahneul / Blended Garlic (page 49)
- 4 (61/70-size) shrimp (meaning 61 to 70 are equal to a pound), heads and shells on
- ½ cup / 60g combination of sliced (about 1 inch / 2.5cm) zucchini, onions, mushrooms, and Korean radish
- 1 (11-oz / 312g) package extra-soft tofu Toasted sesame oil, for finishing Handful of green onions, green and white parts, chopped, for garnish
- 1 small egg

TO MAKE THE SOON TOFU

1 Place a clay pot over high heat. Add ½ cup / 120ml of the beef broth, the dadaegi, and garlic and stir. Cook until the broth is at a full boil and the dadaegi has fully dissolved, turning the broth bright red, about 5 minutes.

2 Add the shrimp, vegetables, and remaining ½ cup / 120ml beef broth. Continue to boil until the shrimp are cooked through—they should be firm and no longer translucent—and the vegetables are tender and cooked through, 2 to 3 minutes.

3 Add ½ package of tofu. Use a spoon to divide the tofu into smaller pieces, then stir to distribute the pieces, doing so gently to avoid breaking up the tofu any further. Be sure to stir the bottom of the pot, too, to prevent burning.

4 Stop stirring and bring the soon tofu back to a boil. Add another ¼ package of tofu to the pot, dividing it into smaller pieces with your spoon, and stir gently again. Bring the pot to a boil, then add the remaining ¼ package of tofu and stir.

5 Cook until the center of the soon tofu is at a rapid boil, about 10 minutes. Finish with a splash of sesame oil and the green onions. Crack the egg into the pot. Allow the egg to cook, undisturbed, until the whites are firm and the yolk is as done as you'd like.

6 Serve boiling hot on a trivet at the table along with the banchan, kimchi, and any shared platter you may have prepared.

QUICK REFERENCE:
QUANTITIES FOR 4 CLAY POTS

- 4 cups / 950ml beef broth (page 42 or 44) or store-bought
- 8 tablespoons / 160g Dadaegi / Seasoned Red Pepper Paste (page 49), or to taste (see How Spicy? on page 77)
- 4 teaspoons Gahreun Mahneul / Blended Garlic (page 49)
- 16 (61/70-sized) shrimp (meaning 61 to 70 are equal to a pound), heads and shells on
- 2 cups / 240g combination of sliced (about 1 inch / 2.5cm) zucchini, onions, mushrooms, and Korean radish
- 4 (11-oz/ 312g) packages extra-soft tofu
  Toasted sesame oil, for finishing
- ½ bunch green onions, green and white parts, chopped, for garnish
- 4 small eggs

OJINGEO KONGNAMUL SOON TOFU

오징어 콩나물 순두부

Squid and Soybean Sprout Soon Tofu

Serves 1

When I was in Korea a few years ago, it was wintertime, and I noticed everyone around me eating steaming-hot bowls of soybean sprout soup. The soup was said to help you avoid catching a cold or, if you were sick, to provide comfort and nourishment. I knew right then that I wanted to incorporate soybean sprouts into a delicious, healthy soon tofu stew, and that I wanted to include squid, too, because the sprouts pair perfectly with the squid's clean, mild flavors. I like to make this soon tofu spicy, which means adding plenty of dadaegi; the heat of the red pepper paste brings out the squid's sweet flavors of the sea. If you love squid, feel free to add more than what I call for.

For 1 individual soon tofu

- 1 cup / 240ml homemade beef broth (page 42 or 44) or store-bought
- 2 tablespoons Dadaegi / Seasoned Red Pepper Paste (page 49), or to taste (see How Spicy? on page 77)
- 1 teaspoon Gahreun Mahneul / Blended Garlic (page 49)
- ½ cup (about ¼ lb / 113g) squid, cleaned and sliced into bite-sized pieces
- ½ cup / 60g combination of sliced (about 1 inch / 2.5cm) zucchini, onions, mushrooms (button, cremini, trumpet, or oyster), and Korean radish
- ½ cup / 40g soybean sprouts, rinsed
- 1 (11-oz / 312g) package extra-soft tofu
  Toasted sesame oil, for finishing
  Handful of green onions, green and white parts, chopped, for garnish
- 1 small egg

TO MAKE THE SOON TOFU

1 Place a clay pot over high heat. Add ½ cup / 120ml of the beef broth, the dadaegi, and garlic and stir. Cook until the broth is at a full boil and the dadaegi has fully dissolved, coloring the broth bright red, about 5 minutes.

2 Add the squid, vegetables, sprouts, and remaining ½ cup / 120ml beef broth. Continue to boil until the vegetables are tender and cooked through, 10 to 15 minutes.

3 Add ½ package of tofu. Use a spoon to divide the tofu into smaller pieces, then stir to distribute the pieces, doing so gently to avoid breaking up the tofu any further. Be sure to stir the bottom of the pot, too, to prevent burning.

4 Stop stirring and bring the soon tofu back to a boil. Add another ¼ package of tofu to the pot, dividing it into smaller pieces with your spoon, and stir gently again. Bring the pot to a boil, then add remaining package of tofu and stir.

5 Cook until the center of the soon tofu is at a rapid boil, about 10 minutes. Finish with a splash of sesame oil and the green onions. Crack the egg into the pot. Allow the egg to cook, undisturbed, until the whites are firm and the yolk is as done as you'd like.

6 Serve boiling hot on a trivet at the table along with the banchan, kimchi, and any shared platter you may have prepared.

QUICK REFERENCE:
QUANTITIES FOR 4 CLAY POTS

- 4 cups / 950ml homemade beef broth (page 42 or 44) or store-bought
- 8 tablespoons / 160g Dadaegi / Seasoned Red Pepper Paste (page 49), or to taste (see How Spicy? on page 77)
- 4 teaspoons Gahreun Mahneul / Blended Garlic (page 49)
- 2 cups / 454g squid, cleaned and sliced into bite-sized pieces
- 2 cups / 240g combination of sliced (about 1 inch / 2.5cm) zucchini, onions, mushrooms, and Korean radish
- 2 cups / 160g soybean sprouts, rinsed
- 4 (11-oz / 312g) packages extra-soft tofu
  Toasted sesame oil, for finishing
- ½ bunch green onions, green and white parts, chopped, for garnish
- 4 small eggs

YAHCHAE SOON TOFU

야채 순두부

Vegetable Soon Tofu

Serves 1

Most soon tofu use a beef or seafood broth as the base, but that's not always necessary. You can use water and still make a delicious, flavorful soon tofu. For this vegetable-rich version, I use an assortment of zucchini, onions, mushrooms, and Korean radish. If you plan to include mushrooms I suggest button, cremini, trumpet, or oyster mushrooms (and not shiitake mushrooms, as their stronger flavor will overwhelm the broth). The vegetables are especially good with the heat and flavor of the dadaegi, so if you can tolerate it, I recommend serving this soon tofu spicy.

For 1 individual soon tofu

1	cup / 240ml water
2¼	tablespoons Dadaegi / Seasoned Red Pepper Paste (page 49), or to taste (see How Spicy? on page 77)
1	teaspoon Gahreun Mahneul / Blended Garlic (page 49)
1	cup / 120g combination of sliced (about 1 inch / 2.5cm) zucchini, onions, mushrooms, and Korean radish
1	(11-oz / 312g) package extra-soft tofu
	Toasted sesame oil, for finishing
	Handful of green onions, green and white parts, chopped, for finishing
1	small egg

TO MAKE THE SOON TOFU

1 Place a clay pot over high heat. Add ½ cup / 120ml of the water, the dadaegi, and garlic and stir. Cook until the broth is at a full boil and the dadaegi has fully dissolved, turning the broth bright red, about 5 minutes.

2 Add the vegetables and the remaining ½ cup / 120ml water. Continue to boil until the radish is tender, 4 to 6 minutes.

3 Add ½ package of tofu. Use a spoon to divide the tofu into smaller pieces, then stir to distribute the pieces, doing so gently to avoid breaking up the tofu any further. Be sure to stir the bottom of the pot, too, to prevent burning.

4 Stop stirring and bring the soon tofu back to a boil. Add another ¼ package of tofu to the pot, dividing it into smaller pieces with your spoon, and stir gently again. Bring the pot to a boil, then add the remaining ¼ package of tofu and stir.

5 Cook until the center of the soon tofu is at a rapid boil, about 10 minutes.

6 Finish with a splash of the sesame oil and the green onions. Crack the egg into the pot. Allow the egg to cook, undisturbed, until the whites are firm and the yolk is as done as you'd like.

7 Serve boiling hot on a trivet at the table along with the banchan, kimchi, and any shared platter you may have prepared.

▶▶▶ **To make this soon tofu vegetarian,** use the vegetarian version of Dadaegi (page 49).

▶▶▶ **To make this soon tofu vegan,** use the vegetarian version of Dadaegi (page 49) and omit the egg.

QUICK REFERENCE:
QUANTITIES FOR 4 CLAY POTS

- 4 cups / 950ml water
- 9 tablespoons / 180g Dadaegi / Seasoned Red Pepper Paste (page 49), or to taste (see How Spicy? on page 77)
- 4 teaspoons Gahreun Mahneul / Blended Garlic (page 49)
- 4 cups / 480g combination of sliced (about 1 inch / 2.5cm) zucchini, onions, mushrooms, and Korean radish
- 4 (11-oz / 312g) packages extra-soft tofu
  Toasted sesame oil, for finishing
- ½ bunch green onions, green and white parts, chopped, for garnish
- 4 small eggs

김 순두부

Seaweed Soon Tofu

Serves 1

Today, soon tofu chigae is the most common way to enjoy extra-soft tofu, but before it was popular to serve it in a stew, extra-soft tofu was served more simply, with just some seaweed and soy sauce. This seaweed chigae recalls those times and lets the tofu shine. The broth here is flavored with just a sprinkle of salt and some garlic (and no dadaegi). I take such a light touch with this stew because most of the seasoning comes from the freshly toasted seaweed and a seasoned soy sauce, both of which are served alongside the soon tofu. For the perfect bite, spoon some soon tofu over rice, sprinkle a bit of seaweed on top, then add just enough tofu sauce to complement the flavor of the tofu.

For 1 individual soon tofu

- 2 to 3 sheets unoiled, unsalted seaweed
- 1 cup / 240ml homemade beef broth (page 42 or 44) or store-bought
- 1 teaspoon Gahreun Mahneul / Blended Garlic (page 49)
  Sea salt
- 1½ (11-oz / 312g) packages extra-soft tofu
  Toasted sesame oil, for finishing
  Tofu Sauce (recipe follows), for serving

TO TOAST THE SEAWEED

Working with one sheet of seaweed at a time, place the seaweed directly over a low or medium flame. Hold the sheet by the edge and flip it a few times to make sure each side is crisp and lightly toasted (alternatively, use a pair of tongs to flip the sheets). It will take just 1 to 2 minutes. You can also toast the sheet in a small ungreased skillet over low heat, flipping it often until it's lightly toasted. Repeat with the remaining sheets. Once the sheets are cool, tear them into bite-sized pieces and place them in a small serving bowl. Set aside.

TO MAKE THE SOON TOFU

1 Place a clay pot over high heat. Add ½ cup / 120ml of the beef broth, the garlic, and a pinch of salt and stir. Cook until the broth is at a full boil, about 5 minutes.

2 Add ½ package of tofu. Use a spoon to divide the tofu into smaller pieces, then stir to distribute the pieces, doing so gently to avoid breaking up the tofu any further. Be sure to stir the bottom of the pot, too, to prevent burning. Then add the remaining ½ cup / 120ml beef broth.

3 Stop stirring and bring the soon tofu back to a boil. Add ½ package of tofu to the pot, dividing it into smaller pieces with your spoon, and stir gently again. Bring the pot to a boil, then add the remaining ½ package of tofu and stir.

4 Cook until the center of the soon tofu is at a rapid boil, about 10 minutes. Finish with a splash of sesame oil.

CONTINUED

5 Carefully transfer the pot, still boiling, from the stove to the table and place on a trivet or other heatproof setting. Serve the toasted seaweed sheets and tofu sauce in separate bowls along with steamed rice and other dishes. Be careful to use the tofu sauce in moderation since you need only enough to accentuate the tofu; the saltiness of the sauce should not make the soon tofu salty as well.

QUICK REFERENCE:
QUANTITIES FOR 4 CLAY POTS

8-12 toasted seaweed sheets (for serving)
4 cups / 950ml homemade beef broth (page 42 or 44) or store-bought
4 teaspoons Gahreun Mahneul / Blended Garlic (page 49)
Sea salt
6 (11-oz / 312g) packages extra-soft tofu
Toasted sesame oil, for finishing
Tofu Sauce, for serving

Tofu Sauce

Makes about ½ cup / 150g

This sauce will make enough to accompany four servings of the Seaweed Soon Tofu. Leftovers, if any, can be stored in an airtight container and placed in the refrigerator for up to three days.

3 tablespoons soy sauce
3 tablespoons rice cooking wine
1 tablespoon toasted sesame seeds (page 51)
1 tablespoon toasted sesame oil
1½ teaspoons granulated sugar
2 tablespoons chopped green onions, green and white parts
1 tablespoon chopped bell pepper, any color (optional)

Place 3 tablespoons water in a small bowl and add the soy sauce, cooking wine, sesame seeds, sesame oil, sugar, green onions, and bell pepper (if using). Stir to combine, then it's ready to serve.

Soybean Paste Soon Tofu

Serves 1

Doenjang chigae (soybean paste stew) is very popular in Korea, and it usually includes firm tofu along with other fillings. I wanted to make a soon tofu version of that chigae, because I think the restrained texture and flavor of extra-soft tofu better complements the more subtle, nuanced notes of the soybean paste. To fully appreciate the doenjang, I also limit the amount of dadaegi I add and keep this one on the milder side. If you would like more heat, add a few slices of jalapeño rather than more dadaegi, since the latter introduces more salt to the broth. While I personally like to use a beef broth for this you can also use my Anchovy and Dashi Broth (page 48) or water. While the recipe instructs you to make the soon tofu as four individual servings, you'll be marinating the short rib trimmings in one large batch.

For 1 individual soon tofu

- 1 cup / 240ml homemade beef broth (page 42 or 44), Anchovy and Dashi Broth (page 48), or store-bought
- 3¾ teaspoons doenjang (fermented soybean paste)
- ½ teaspoon Dadaegi / Seasoned Red Pepper Paste (page 49)
  Sliced jalapeños (optional)
- 1 teaspoon Gahreun Mahneul / Blended Garlic (page 49)
- ¼ cup / 115g marinated short rib trimmings
- ½ cup / 60g combination of sliced (1 inch / 2.5cm) zucchini, onions, mushrooms (button, cremini, trumpet, or oyster), and Korean radish
- 1 (11-oz / 312g) package extra-soft tofu
  Toasted sesame oil, for finishing
  Handful of green onions, green and white parts, chopped, for garnish
- 1 small egg

TO MAKE THE SOON TOFU

1 Place a clay pot over high heat. Add ½ cup / 120ml of the beef broth, the doenjang, dadaegi, jalapeños (if using), garlic, marinated trimmings, and vegetables and stir. Cook until the soup is at a full boil, the beef is cooked all the way through and no longer pink, and the doenjang and dadaegi have fully dissolved, turning the broth a deep tan color, about 5 minutes.

2 Add ½ package of tofu and the remaining ½ cup / 120ml beef broth. Use a spoon to divide the tofu into smaller pieces, then stir to distribute the pieces, doing so gently to avoid breaking up the tofu any further. Be sure to stir the bottom of the pot, too, to prevent burning, and skim any fat or other impurities that rise to the surface.

3 Stop stirring and bring the soon tofu back to a boil. Add another ¼ package of tofu to the pot, dividing it into smaller pieces with your spoon, and stir gently again. Bring the pot to a boil, then add the remaining ¼ package of tofu and stir.

CONTINUED

4 Cook until the center of the soon tofu is at a rapid boil, about 10 minutes. Finish with a splash of sesame oil and the green onions. Crack the egg into the pot. Allow the egg to cook, undisturbed, until the whites are firm and the yolk is as done as you'd like.

5 Serve boiling hot on a trivet at the table along with the banchan, kimchi, and any shared platter you may have prepared.

▶▶▶ **To make this soon tofu vegetarian,** use the vegetarian version of Dadaegi (page 49).

▶▶▶ **To make this soon tofu vegan,** use the vegetarian version of Dadaegi (page 49) and omit the egg.

Marinated Short Rib Trimmings

Makes enough for 4 servings of soon tofu

1	cup (about ½ lb / 225g) short rib trimmings, sliced into bite-sized pieces
½	teaspoon Gahreun Mahneul / Blended Garlic (page 49)
½	teaspoon toasted sesame oil
½	teaspoon sea salt

TO MARINATE THE TRIMMINGS: In a medium bowl, combine the short rib trimmings, garlic, sesame oil, and salt and marinate for 20 to 30 minutes.

**QUICK REFERENCE:
QUANTITIES FOR 4 CLAY POTS**

4	cups / 950ml homemade beef broth (page 42 or 44), Anchovy and Dashi Broth (page 48), or store-bought
5	tablespoons / 112g doenjang (fermented soybean paste)
2	teaspoons Dadaegi / Seasoned Red Pepper Paste (page 49)
	Sliced jalapeños (optional)
4	teaspoons Gahreun Mahneul / Blended Garlic (page 49)
2	cups / 450g marinated short rib trimmings
2	cups / 240g combination of sliced (1 inch / 2.5cm) zucchini, onions, mushrooms (button, cremini, trumpet, or oyster), and Korean radishes
4	(11-oz / 312g) packages extra-soft tofu
½	bunch green onions, green and white parts, chopped, for garnish
	Toasted sesame oil, for finishing
4	small eggs

HOW SPICY TO MAKE YOUR SOON TOFU?

The spice level for most of my soon tofu can easily be adjusted to suit your own personal preference simply by adjusting how much dadaegi / Seasoned Red Pepper Paste (page 49) you add to the clay pot. Use the table below to make your soon tofu exactly as spicy (or not spicy) as you'd like. (Note that my Gogi Kimchi Soon Tofu / Beef or Pork Kimchi Soon Tofu, Geem Soon Tofu / Seaweed Soon Tofu, and Doenjang Soon Tofu / Soybean Paste Soon Tofu are omitted from this table; refer to those recipes for specific recommendations about their spice levels.)

SPICE LEVEL	AMOUNT OF DADAEGI (PER SINGLE CLAY POT) TO ADD
Not Spicy	Do not add any dadaegi, but taste the soon tofu before serving and add more salt if needed.
Mild	1 to 2 teaspoons, plus salt to taste
Medium	2 tablespoons
Spicy	2 tablespoons plus 1 teaspoon
Extra Spicy	2 tablespoons plus 1 teaspoon, plus sliced jalapeños

The Largest Koreatown in America

There are Koreatowns all over the United States, but it is right here in Los Angeles that you will find the largest population of Koreans outside of Seoul and, at nearly 3 square miles / 7.8 square km, the biggest Koreatown in America.

Koreatown is located just a few miles west of downtown Los Angeles in the central part of the city. It is one of the most densely populated neighborhoods in LA, and despite its name, it is also one of the most diverse: Bangladeshis, Filipinos, and African Americans all call Koreatown home. The majority of the population is actually Latino, most of whom have Mexican, Salvadoran, and Guatemalan origins. I learned enough Spanish to be able to communicate with my staff and customers, and many of them learned some Korean, too!

Koreans have been moving to Los Angeles since the early 1900s, setting up church organizations and other associations downtown and around the University of Southern California (USC), which is just south of downtown. Due to restrictive housing covenants, the neighborhood around USC was one of the few areas where Koreans could live. It's still sometimes referred to as Old Koreatown.

The neighborhood that would become today's Koreatown was just a few miles north of Old Koreatown, and between the 1920s and 1950s, it was actually a hot spot where Hollywood stars partied and socialized. If you walk or drive around Koreatown today, you can see some of the landmarks from those bygone days.

In the 1950s, Koreans began moving to Los Angeles in larger numbers, and the Korean population increased even more after the Immigration and Naturalization Act of 1965 opened the country's borders to a greater number of immigrants from countries outside of Europe. My uncle was among those early immigrants. He came to Los Angeles as a graduate student to study pharmacy at USC.

By then, housing restrictions had been lifted, and the Hollywood crowd had moved west, leaving behind a neighborhood in economic decline. New immigrants saw this vacancy as an opportunity, and in 1971, when there were only about 5,700 Koreans in Los Angeles, a Korean grocery called Olympic Market opened on Olympic Boulevard. Soon, a cluster of accounting services, restaurants, and other Korean-owned businesses opened nearby. That was the beginning of the Koreatown we know today.

When I arrived in Los Angeles in 1977, Koreatown was still fairly small, but it was bustling with activity. One of the first places I visited was Olympic Market, and I will never forget it. That was where I tasted honeydew and cantaloupe and Alaskan crab legs for the very first time. They were so delicious! It was also at that market that I had my first taste of LA-style galbi. I loved tasting all these new flavors and couldn't stop eating.

By 1980, there were about 33,000 Koreans in LA, and Koreatown was very quickly becoming the center of Korean culture for all of Southern California, if not the United States. Indeed, in the nine years between my arrival in Los Angeles in 1977 and the opening of Beverly Soon Tofu in 1986, Koreatown changed significantly. By then, the city had already designated the area as Koreatown, and Korean-owned businesses pushed the boundaries of the neighborhood far past its original few blocks around Olympic Market. More restaurants began to open, offering a greater variety of Korean food and often specializing in very specific dishes like beef bone broth, and Korean BBQ. Bigger markets opened, selling produce, seafood, and other items imported from Korea.

But there were challenges, too. The county's health department inspects restaurants to ensure compliance with food safety regulations, which is unquestionably important. But many inspectors had little experience with Korean food. Early on, for example, when I made my own tofu for Beverly Soon Tofu, my inspector had never seen a restaurant make tofu from scratch before. More generally, some of our cooking processes, like fermenting vegetables to make kimchi, differed from what the inspectors were familiar with, so it was often a challenge for both sides to understand each other. The same year I opened the restaurant, I became the vice president of Koreatown's restaurant association and met often with the health department to promote cultural literacy and greater understanding for our mutual benefit.

But the most difficult moment for Koreatown came in 1992, when four Los Angeles Police Department officers were acquitted of charges related to the beating of Rodney King. That day, I was told by the National Guard to close my restaurant early. I did so and went home and hoped for the best. Meanwhile, Los Angeles erupted in anger over this injustice, and Koreatown was in flames for four days. I was very fortunate that Beverly Soon Tofu did not suffer major damage, but many, many others were not as lucky.

In a testament to our neighborhood's resilience, Koreatown sprang back in the following decade with many businesses rebuilding literally from the ground up. By the early 2010s, the neighborhood, with new restaurants, hotels, and shopping malls, was just starting to become trendy. And then, in 2013, Anthony Bourdain visited my restaurant with Roy Choi to film an episode of *Parts Unknown,* and suddenly there was a whole new audience who wanted to try my soon tofu and explore Koreatown. That was a real turning point for the neighborhood; soon after that, the *New York Times, Vogue,* and other media drew even more national attention to the neighborhood.

Nowadays, trends from Korea make it to Koreatown in no time at all, and the neighborhood is dynamic and constantly changing. That is even more true now, as COVID-19 has upended everything.

As for the pandemic, we experienced a lot of uncertainty in 1992, but nothing like in early 2020, when we closed for six weeks before tentatively reopening for takeout. When we closed our doors for good in September 2020, we followed the same path as many other restaurants, including a few that had been open even longer than Beverly Soon Tofu.

Though legacy businesses like mine have not been able to survive the pandemic, I think the future of Koreatown is very bright. There is a new generation of Korean American entrepreneurs, including chefs and restaurateurs, in Koreatown, all of whom have risen up despite the pandemic's challenges, and what I see in them is a passion for their craft. I have no doubt that like me, they are resilient. They are survivors. And they are proud to celebrate what they do, whether it is making food to share with others, making art that celebrates their traditions and beliefs, or building a community that thrives on a strong identity of self. The next generation of Koreatown's entrepreneurs will be just fine. They will succeed. And Koreatown, and Los Angeles, will be all the better for it.

The
Soon
Tofu
Table

Soon tofu is usually just one dish among many in a meal. Rice, of course, is always on the table—it is a must. I prefer short-grain white rice with soon tofu, because I think it is a great backdrop to the stew and allows the clarity and nuances of the tofu and the stew to come through. If you prefer, however, you certainly could serve soon tofu with brown rice.

At Beverly Soon Tofu, I also offered multigrain rice, which is rice mixed with a variety of grains and beans. It is healthy and hearty. Bags of multigrain rice are available at Asian markets. If you choose multigrain rice, be sure to read the instructions, since it usually needs to be presoaked before cooking.

The other dishes typically served with soon tofu—and every Korean meal, in fact—are banchan and kimchi. Both are small side dishes that offer a variety of flavors to round out your meal. If you and your guests are especially hungry or would like even more variety, make a full spread by adding a large platter (page 175) to share with the table, too.

BEVERLY SOON TOFU'S BANCHAN

To give you a few ideas to start with, below are some of my favorite banchan to have with soon tofu.

- Mu Saeng Chae / Matchstick Radishes (page 90)

- Gamja Jorim / Braised Potatoes in Soy Sauce (page 106)

- Kongnamul Muchim / Soybean Sprouts (page 91)

- Oh Eeh Muchim / Sweet and Tangy Cucumbers (page 93)

- Kkakdoogi Kimchi / Radish Kimchi (page 141) and/or Spicy Napa Cabbage Kimchi (page 130)

Banchan

From refreshingly tangy cucumbers to hearty beef braised in soy sauce, these banchan are delicious with almost everything, especially with soon tofu.

Pick a few banchan that will stay on the table throughout the meal. When it comes to selecting banchan, there are no rules, but I do suggest that you aim for variety and balance. Have a mix of cold and warm banchan, for example, and if much of the meal is heavy on meat, prepare a few vegetable banchan. Everything should be in harmony.

Having a colorful array of banchan will keep things visually interesting. Being mindful of the presentation and arrangement of the banchan on the table is just as important; ideally, the colors of the dishes will complement each other rather than clash.

Consider the banchan serving sizes listed as mere guidelines. How many any one particular banchan will serve depends on how many other side dishes you're serving and what the other, larger dishes are. If you have very spicy soon tofu, for example, expect your guests to reach for the cool soybean sprouts or the refreshing radish banchan many times!

Banchan with lightly seasoned fresh vegetables are best the day they're made, but most other banchan will store well. Leftover banchan can also be tossed into bibimbap (see page 180) or another rice bowl for a quick meal.

One final recommendation: when you cook for a party, notice which banchan need to be constantly refilled. That will tell you that you have paired these dishes well with the meal, or it may indicate that these are crowd favorites—or both!

MAT GANJANG

맛간장

Seasoned Soy Sauce

Makes about 2 cups / 480ml

This seasoned soy sauce is used in many of my banchan, as well as dishes like my Braised Fish with Radish and Vegetables (page 121), Braised Spicy Pork Ribs (page 206), and Soy-Marinated BBQ Pork Ribs (page 208).

- 1 cup / 240ml soy sauce
- ¾ cup / 150g granulated sugar, plus more to taste
- ¾ cup / 240g light corn syrup, plus more to taste

1 Combine 1 cup / 240ml water with the soy sauce, sugar, and corn syrup in a small pot. Turn the heat to high and stir continuously as you bring the mixture to a boil, then reduce the temperature to medium and simmer for about 5 minutes. Taste. If you'd like it sweeter, add more sugar or corn syrup, a little bit at a time, until it's as sweet as you'd like.

2 Turn off the heat and remove the pot from the stove to cool. Once cooled, the sauce is ready to be used. Leftovers can be stored in an airtight container in the fridge for up to 1 month.

VEGETARIAN, VEGAN

MAEUN YANGNUM

매운 양념

Spicy Red Pepper Marinade

Makes about ⅔ cup / 160g

Maeun yangnum is a staple in my kitchen. It's used in many of the banchan recipes, and it is also a very versatile marinade. If you're not sure how to prepare meat and vegetables, for example, you can toss them in this and make a meal of it. I also like to use it as a stir-fry sauce in my Spicy Stir-Fried Squid with Vegetables (page 198) or to braise a chicken (see page 209). Once made, it will keep very well for a few weeks in an airtight container in your refrigerator, so make a big batch so you'll always have some on hand to make easy, quick meals.

- 2 tablespoons Dadaegi / Seasoned Red Pepper Paste (page 49)
- 2 tablespoons light corn syrup, plus more to taste
- 4½ teaspoons granulated sugar, plus more to taste
- 1 tablespoon gochujang
- 1 tablespoon coarse gochugaru
- 1 tablespoon rice cooking wine
- 1 tablespoon fish sauce
- 1 tablespoon Mat Ganjang / Seasoned Soy Sauce (left)
- 1½ teaspoons sea salt
- ½ teaspoon ground black pepper

Using a spoon or a whisk, mix the dadaegi, corn syrup, sugar, gochujang, gochugaru, cooking wine, fish sauce, seasoned soy sauce, salt, and black pepper in a small bowl with 2 tablespoons water until incorporated. The marinade is now ready to be used for cooking. Place any leftovers in an airtight container and store in the refrigerator for 4 to 6 weeks.

GAHREUN SENGGANG
갈은 생강

Blended Ginger

Makes about 2 cups / 400g

Ginger isn't used in Korean cooking as often as garlic, but I still find it very useful to spend a little bit of time every few weeks preparing a batch of this blended ginger. Similarly to the way I blend garlic with water (see page 49), I combine fresh ginger and water and store the blend in my fridge. Then, rather than peeling and mincing knobs of ginger every time I need it for a dish, I pull out this jar instead. The flavor of this blended ginger is milder than sliced ginger, making it an easy addition to many banchan and kimchi. It will keep in an airtight container in the refrigerator for up to one month. Alternatively, pour the blended ginger into an ice cube tray and keep it in the freezer for up to six months. When you need ginger, all you need to do is pop out a cube; its flavor will keep, and it will be the perfect portion size for most of your needs.

8 oz / 225g fresh ginger, unpeeled

Place the ginger in a large bowl and add enough water to cover (if necessary, you can cut the ginger pieces to fit into your bowl). Soak for at least 1 hour to soften. Drain the water, then peel the ginger and slice it into 1-inch / 2.5cm pieces. Set aside a few slices, then place the remainder in a blender (or a container with tall sides if you're using an immersion blender). Add 1 cup / 240ml water and blend until smooth, then check the consistency: it should very thinly coat the back of a spoon. If it's too thick, add more water, a tablespoon at a time, until it thins out. If it's too watery, add the reserved ginger, a slice at a time, and blend. It can be used immediately.

MU SAENG CHAE
무생채

Matchstick Radishes

Serves 4 to 6

The crisp, bright flavor of these radishes is a perfect complement to Korean BBQ or any other meaty dish. Use Korean radishes, which are available at Korean and other Asian markets. When shopping, bigger isn't necessarily better, but you also want to avoid very small or thin radishes. Instead, look for ones that are plump and firm.

1	medium-to-large mu (Korean radish), about 1 lb / 450g
3	tablespoons white vinegar
2	tablespoons granulated sugar
1½	teaspoons sea salt
1½	teaspoons Gahreun Mahneul / Blended Garlic (page 49)
¼	teaspoon Gahreun Senggang / Blended Ginger (page 89)

1 Peel the radish if the skin is especially thick or fibrous, then slice into rounds about ⅛ inch / 3mm thick. Stack the rounds and slice them into matchsticks (use a mandoline if you have one). Set aside.

2 In a large bowl, combine the vinegar, sugar, salt, garlic, and ginger. Add the radishes and use your hands to coat them with the mixture, massaging them lightly as you do so to ensure they are evenly and thoroughly coated.

3 Place the radishes in an airtight container and refrigerate for at least 6 hours, then serve.

▶▶▶ **To make this banchan spicy,** add 2 tablespoons gochugaru, 1½ teaspoons toasted sesame oil, and 1½ teaspoons toasted sesame seeds (page 51) to the mixture before adding the radishes.

▶▶▶ **For a delightful combination, add squid to this banchan.** You can pick up a whole cooked squid or boil 1 whole squid until it turns opaque, then place it in an ice bath. Pat it dry, then thinly slice the cold cooked squid and add it to the radish mixture. Mix well before serving.

VEGETARIAN, VEGAN, GLUTEN-FREE

콩나물 무침

Soybean Sprouts

Serves 4 to 6

We always have soybean sprouts in my house. They're inexpensive, full of vitamin C, and are such a big part of Korean cooking that I can't imagine a Korean meal without them. This classic banchan allows the sprouts to shine without being overshadowed by other powerful flavors. They are great as part of a meal, as a snack on their own, or when added to a dish like bibimbap for texture. When shopping, avoid sprouts that have turned green, since that's an indication they're not fresh. Instead, look for white sprouts with bright yellow heads and thick, firm stems (thin stems will become leathery when cooked). Some like to trim the root for aesthetic reasons, but I prefer to keep the roots intact to take advantage of all their nutritional value.

- 4 cups / 320g soybean sprouts, rinsed
- 1 teaspoon sea salt
- 2 tablespoons chopped green onions, green and white parts
- 1 tablespoon toasted sesame oil
- 1½ teaspoons Gahreun Mahneul / Blended Garlic (page 49)
- 1½ teaspoons toasted sesame seeds (page 51)
- 1 teaspoon coarse gochugaru (optional)
- ¼ teaspoon ground black pepper (optional)

1 Place a medium pot over high heat. Add the soybean sprouts with enough water to cover plus ½ teaspoon of the salt. Boil the sprouts, uncovered, for 3 to 4 minutes, then toss the sprouts and continue to boil for another 3 to 4 minutes to ensure they are evenly cooked.

2 While the sprouts are boiling, fill a large bowl with water and ice cubes and place it next to the sink.

3 After the sprouts are cooked, drain and rinse them in cold tap water, then drop them into the ice bath. Soak until they're cold to the touch, about 5 minutes.

4 Drain and squeeze the excess liquid from the sprouts, then transfer them to a large bowl. Add the green onions, sesame oil, garlic, sesame seeds, gochugaru (if using), the remaining ½ teaspoon salt, and the black pepper (if using). Using your hands, combine everything until all ingredients are well incorporated. It's ready to serve. Leftovers can be stored in an airtight container in the refrigerator for up to 3 days.

VEGETARIAN, VEGAN, GLUTEN-FREE

Sweet and Tangy Cucumbers

Serves 4 to 6

This is a classic banchan that works with a variety of cucumbers, including English (also called hothouse) cucumbers. When shopping for cucumbers, look for deeply green ones labeled extra fancy or ones that are smaller in size with thin skins. Pickling and Persian cucumbers will also work when they're in season. Outside of their season, pickling cucumbers tend to have skin that's too thick for this banchan, and Persian cucumbers will lose their crisp texture and color too quickly. I often make this banchan for both my daughters when they want an acidic, spicy, tangy side dish to complement my richer and heavier dishes, like galbi or other beef dishes.

The cucumbers should be sliced quite thinly, so I suggest using a mandoline if you have one. Because the cucumbers will lose their crispness over time, these are best eaten within a day after they're made. That said, everyone will want seconds and thirds of this banchan, so you don't have to worry about leftovers: There won't be any left to store!

← (clockwise from top left): Matchstick Radishes (page 90), Sweet and Tangy Cucumbers, Soybean Sprouts (page 91), and Sautéed Zucchini (page 96).

- 2 to 3 cucumbers, thinly sliced (about 4 cups / 480g)
- 1 teaspoon sea salt
- ¼ cup / 60ml white vinegar, plus more to taste
- ¼ cup / 50g granulated sugar, plus more to taste
- 2 tablespoons Gahreun Mahneul / Blended Garlic (page 49)
- 1 teaspoon Gahreun Senggang / Blended Ginger (page 89), plus more to taste
- 2 teaspoons toasted sesame oil
- 1 tablespoon toasted sesame seeds (page 51)

1 Place the sliced cucumbers in a large bowl and add the salt. Mix, then set aside for 15 to 20 minutes to season the cucumbers and allow them to release their liquid. Drain in a colander but do not rinse. Use your hands to gently squeeze out the excess liquid. Set aside.

2 While the cucumbers drain, wipe the bowl dry and add the vinegar, sugar, garlic, ginger, sesame oil, and sesame seeds. Gently mix all the ingredients together with a spoon or by hand until incorporated, then add the cucumbers. Taste. Add an additional ¼ teaspoon ginger if you'd like, or ¼ teaspoon sugar for more sweetness; for more tang, add up to another tablespoon of vinegar. The cucumbers will taste even better after sitting in an airtight container for a few hours or overnight in the fridge. When you store the cucumbers, be sure to keep them in their liquid, since that will keep the slices crispy and refreshing.

VEGETARIAN, VEGAN, GLUTEN-FREE

MAEUN OH EEH MUCHIM

매운오이무침

Spicy Cucumbers

Serves 4

These cucumbers can be served as soon as you make them, but they will taste even better after they've had some time to absorb the flavors of the marinade. That said, I suggest serving the cucumbers within two days. After that, they will become soft and lose their crispness.

10	to 12 Persian cucumbers
1½	teaspoons sea salt
2	tablespoons white vinegar
4½	teaspoons coarse gochugaru
1	tablespoon chopped green onions, green and white parts
1	tablespoon toasted sesame seeds (page 51)
1	tablespoon toasted sesame oil
1	tablespoon light corn syrup
2	teaspoons granulated sugar
1½	teaspoons Gahreun Mahneul / Blended Garlic (page 49)
1	teaspoon fish sauce
¼	teaspoon ground black pepper

1 Trim the cucumbers, quarter them lengthwise, then cut into 1-inch / 2.5cm pieces.

2 Place the cucumbers in a large bowl. Sprinkle the salt over the pieces, then add the vinegar. Stir to mix, then set aside for 15 to 20 minutes. Drain the liquid from the cucumbers and transfer to a colander set over a large bowl. Place a heavy weight, like a pan or a plate, directly on top of the cucumbers and set aside again, this time for 10 to 15 minutes. Drain any excess liquid and pat the cucumbers dry with a paper towel.

3 Wipe the bowl dry and add the cucumbers, gochugaru, green onions, sesame seeds, sesame oil, corn syrup, sugar, garlic, fish sauce, and black pepper. Mix everything with your hands, making sure all ingredients are well incorporated. The cucumbers are now ready to serve. To store, place the cucumbers in an airtight container in the refrigerator for up to 2 days.

▶▶▶ Although the fish sauce gives a bit of umami to the cucumbers, it can be omitted if you don't have any on hand or would prefer to make a vegetarian or vegan version. If you leave out the fish sauce, increase the salt by ½ teaspoon.

HOBAK NAMUL
호박 나물

Sautéed Zucchini

Serves 4 to 6

This combination of zucchini and salted shrimp makes for a delicious banchan. For this recipe, aehobak (Korean zucchini) are best, especially during the summer, when they're in season; they're slightly sweeter and firmer than their Italian counterpart. You can find aehobak at Korean and some Asian markets. If they aren't available, any zucchini or other firm summer squash will work.

1 lb / 450g medium zucchini, preferably aehobak

2 tablespoons vegetable or other neutral oil

1 tablespoon Gahreun Mahneul / Blended Garlic (page 49)

1 tablespoon salted shrimp (page 25)

1½ teaspoons fish sauce

1 teaspoon coarse gochugaru (optional)

½ teaspoon ground black pepper

2 tablespoons chopped green onions, green and white parts

1 tablespoon toasted sesame seeds (page 51)

1 tablespoon toasted sesame oil

1 Slice the zucchini in half lengthwise, then slice each half into ¼-inch / 6mm half-moons. (You should end up with about 4 cups / 480g). Set aside.

2 Place a large heavy-bottomed pan or sauté pan over high heat and add the vegetable oil. When the oil begins to shimmer, add the zucchini, followed by the garlic, salted shrimp, fish sauce, gochugaru (if using), and black pepper. Sauté for about 5 minutes, then pour in ¼ cup / 60ml water and continue to sauté until the zucchini is cooked all the way through. (Some water may remain in the pan even after the zucchini cooks through; that's okay.) Turn off the heat. Add the green onions, sesame seeds, and sesame oil and stir to incorporate. Serve immediately. To store, place the zucchini in an airtight container and keep in the refrigerator. It is best eaten within 3 days.

브로컬리 두부 무침

Broccoli with Tofu

Serves 4 to 6

This is an easy side dish that's colorful and healthy. It's also very customizable: if you don't have broccoli in your fridge or want to add even more vegetables, cauliflower and carrots are excellent. However you make it, be sure to add enough sesame seeds to the mix, as they contribute a distinctly nutty, roasted flavor to the dish. Black sesame seeds, which are nuttier than their white counterparts, offer a beautiful color contrast against the forest green of the blanched broccoli.

- 2 **cups / 200g broccoli florets**
- 2 **teaspoons sea salt**
- 2 **drops of vegetable or other neutral oil**
- 1 **(19-oz / 538g) package firm tofu, preferably House Foods brand**
- ⅔ **cup / 100g sliced (about 1 inch / 2.5cm) red bell pepper (about 1 pepper)**
- ⅔ **cup / 100g sliced (about 1 inch / 2.5cm) yellow bell pepper (about 1 pepper)**
- ⅔ **cup / 80g sliced (about 1 inch / 2.5cm) red onion (about 1 medium onion)**
- ⅔ **cup / 96g sliced (about 1 inch / 2.5cm) imitation crab (4 to 6 sticks)**
- 2 **tablespoons chopped green onions, green and white parts**
- 2 **tablespoons toasted sesame oil**
- 2 **tablespoons toasted sesame seeds (page 51), preferably black sesame seeds**
- 1 **tablespoon Gahreun Mahneul / Blended Garlic (page 49)**
- 1 **teaspoon fish sauce**

1 Place a large pot of water over high heat.

2 While the water is coming to a boil, prepare an ice bath by filling a large bowl with water and ice cubes. Cut the broccoli florets into bite-sized pieces and set aside.

3 When the water reaches a boil, add 1 teaspoon of the salt, the vegetable oil, and then the broccoli florets. Blanch the broccoli for about 30 seconds, then remove with a spider or slotted spoon and place the florets directly into the ice bath for a few minutes, until they're chilled. Transfer the broccoli to a colander set over a bowl or plate and set aside to drain.

4 Place the tofu in another colander set over a bowl. Using a spoon, crumble the tofu until it roughly resembles ground beef, pressing the pieces against the colander as you do so to remove as much liquid as possible.

5 In a large bowl, combine the crumbled tofu, broccoli, bell peppers, red onion, crab, and green onions and mix. Add the sesame oil, sesame seeds, garlic, fish sauce, and the remaining 1 teaspoon salt and mix one more time before serving. Place any leftovers in an airtight container and store in the refrigerator for 2 to 3 days.

Eggplant Banchan Two Ways

Here are two ways to use eggplant for banchan. The first recipe is from my grandmother, who always had eggplant on hand during the summer and liked to steam it for the classic banchan called gaji namul. The second recipe is my own take, where I stir-fry the eggplant pieces with my Mat Ganjang / Seasoned Soy Sauce (page 88). Both use Japanese eggplants, which can be as deeply purple as Italian and American eggplants but are slender in shape and have thinner skins and creamier flesh. You can find them in many supermarkets as well as Asian grocers. When shopping, look for eggplants that are on the smaller, thinner side; those have the softest flesh and will be more delicious when cooked.

GAJI NAMUL

가지 나물

Seasoned Eggplant

Serves 4

- 4 to 6 Japanese eggplants
- 1 tablespoon Gahreun Mahneul / Blended Garlic (page 49)
- 2 teaspoons toasted sesame oil
- 2 teaspoons white vinegar
- 2 teaspoons toasted sesame seeds (page 51)
- 1 teaspoon coarse gochugaru
- 1 teaspoon granulated sugar
- 1 teaspoon sea salt
- 1 teaspoon fish sauce (optional) Ground black pepper
- 2 tablespoons chopped green onions, green and white parts, for garnish

1 Quarter the eggplants and slice them into strips that are about ½ inch / 12mm thick and 3 inches / 7.5cm long. You should have about 4 cups / 480g. Place the eggplant in a steamer basket and steam until tender, about 10 minutes.

2 Meanwhile, combine the garlic, sesame oil, vinegar, gochugaru, sugar, salt, fish sauce (if using), and a pinch of black pepper in a large bowl. Add the cooked eggplant slices and gently stir to combine. Garnish with the green onions and sesame seeds.

VEGETARIAN, VEGAN, GLUTEN-FREE

GAJI BOKKEUM

가지 볶음

Stir-Fried Eggplant

Serves 4

4   to 6 Japanese eggplants
4½ teaspoons toasted sesame oil,
     plus more for finishing
1   tablespoon extra-virgin olive oil
2   tablespoons Mat Ganjang /
     Seasoned Soy Sauce (page 88)
1   tablespoon Gahreun Mahneul /
     Blended Garlic (page 49)
     Ground black pepper, to taste
½   medium yellow onion, sliced
¼   bell pepper or 1 mini bell pepper
     (any color), thinly sliced
2   tablespoons thinly sliced green onions,
     green and white parts, for garnish
2   teaspoons toasted sesame seeds
     (page 51), for garnish

1 Halve the eggplants lengthwise, then slice each half into half-moons about ⅛ inch / 3mm, until you have about 4 cups / 480g. Set aside.

2 Place a large sauté pan over high heat and add the sesame and olive oils. Once the oils are shimmering, add the eggplants and sauté until they begin to soften and color, 1 to 2 minutes, then add 1 tablespoon water and stir. Add the seasoned soy sauce, garlic, and black pepper and sauté for 1 minute. Add the yellow onion and bell pepper and sauté for 2 minutes, or until tender. Remove the pan from the heat and garnish with the green onions and sesame seeds. Finish with a few drops of sesame oil.

VEGETARIAN, VEGAN

(left to right): Seasoned Eggplant (page 98),
Stir-Fried Eggplant (page 99)

Spinach Banchan Two Ways

These recipes offer two different but equally great ways to use spinach. The first is mild and simply seasoned; the second incorporates my Maeun Yangnum / Spicy Red Pepper Marinade (page 88), gochugaru for spice, and Fuji apple slices for sweetness. For both, remember that spinach will shrink considerably when cooked. Because the size of a bunch of spinach varies depending on the time of year and the source, you may need only four bunches if they're large, or you may need five if they're on the smaller side; either way, you're aiming for 1½ cups / 180g of cooked spinach. After blanching the spinach, be sure to wring out as much water as you can, so it can better absorb all the seasonings. If you have leftovers of either banchan, they will keep, refrigerated and covered, for two to three days.

SHIGEUMCHI NAMUL
시금치 나물

Seasoned Spinach

Serves 4 to 6

- 1 teaspoon sea salt
- 2 or 3 drops of vegetable or other neutral oil
- 4 to 5 bunches spinach, washed well
- 2 tablespoons chopped green onions, green and white parts
- 2 tablespoons toasted sesame oil
- 1 tablespoon toasted sesame seeds (page 51)
- 1 tablespoon Gahreun Mahneul / Blended Garlic (page 49)
- 1 teaspoon fish sauce
- ½ teaspoon ground black pepper (optional)

1 Place a large pot of water over high heat. Add ½ teaspoon of the salt and the vegetable oil. Bring to a boil, then drop in the spinach and boil until the spinach is tender, about 1 minute. Drain in a colander and rinse in cold tap water, being sure to rinse the spinach thoroughly to remove any remaining dirt or grit. Use your hands to wring out as much water from the spinach as possible and measure out 1½ cups / 180g. If you have extra, save it for another dish.

2 Squeeze the spinach into a small ball, transfer it to a cutting board, and coarsely chop. Place the chopped spinach in a medium bowl and add the green onions, sesame oil, sesame seeds, garlic, fish sauce, black pepper (if using), and the remaining ½ teaspoon salt. Use your hands to mix everything together. Serve alongside the other dishes in your meal.

MAEUN SHIGEUMCHI NAMUL

매운 시금치 나물

Spicy Seasoned Spinach

Serves 4 to 6

- ½ teaspoon sea salt
- 2 or 3 drops of vegetable or other neutral oil
- 4 to 5 bunches spinach, washed well
- 1 Fuji apple or other firm, sweet apple, thinly sliced
- 2 tablespoons chopped green onions, green and white parts
- 4½ teaspoons Maeun Yangnum / Spicy Red Pepper Marinade (page 88)
- 1 tablespoon Gahreun Mahneul / Blended Garlic (page 49)
- 1 tablespoon white vinegar
- 2 teaspoons toasted sesame seeds (page 51)
- 2 teaspoons toasted sesame oil
- 2 teaspoons coarse gochugaru
- 1 teaspoon fish sauce
  Ground black pepper

1 Place a large pot of water over high heat. Add the salt and vegetable oil. Bring to a boil, then drop in the spinach. Boil until the spinach is tender, about 1 minute. Drain in a colander and rinse in cold tap water, being sure to rinse the spinach thoroughly to remove any remaining dirt or grit. Use your hands to wring out as much water as possible, and measure out 1½ cups / 180g of the cooked spinach. If you have extra, save it for another dish.

2 Squeeze the spinach into a small ball, transfer it to a cutting board, and coarsely chop. Place the chopped spinach in a medium bowl and add the apple, green onions, red pepper marinade, garlic, vinegar, sesame seeds, sesame oil, gochugaru, fish sauce, and a pinch of black pepper. Use your hands to mix everything together. Place it on a small serving dish and serve it with your meal.

감자 볶음

Sautéed Shoestring Potatoes

Serves 4

I used to make this recipe often when I was in high school and college. Back then, I loved cooking when we went camping and took trips to the beach with my family and friends. We didn't have much money, so these potatoes were perfect to make on those outings, since they required just a few inexpensive ingredients and could be cooked over a fire outdoors. I still make gamja bokkeum to this day, and everyone, from kids to adults, still loves them. I sometimes sneak in extra carrots to make them even more nutritious. In Korea, I often added a few slivers of Korean peppers to the pan because I like spiciness; here in the United States, Korean peppers are sometimes available at Korean grocers like H Mart, but jalapeños can be used in their place. With that bit of spice, the potatoes are especially good with a cold beer. The Spam here is optional as well. If you eat meat, it's a delicious addition.

- 2 russet potatoes, peeled
- 1 medium carrot
- ½ medium yellow onion
- 3 or 4 green onions
- 2 tablespoons vegetable or other neutral oil
- 2 oz / 55g Spam, sliced into matchsticks (optional)
- ¾ teaspoon sea salt
- 2 teaspoons Gahreun Mahneul / Blended Garlic (page 49)
- ¼ teaspoon ground black pepper
- ½ Korean chile pepper (or jalapeño), thinly sliced (optional)
- 1 teaspoon toasted sesame seeds (page 51), for garnish

1 Slice the potatoes into rounds ⅛ inch / 3mm thick. Stack the rounds and slice them into ⅛-inch / 3mm strips (use a mandoline if you have one). In a large bowl, soak the sliced potatoes in cold tap water for 10 minutes to release some of their starch, then drain and pat dry with a paper towel.

2 While the potatoes are soaking, slice the carrot, yellow onion, and green onions into matchsticks the same size as the potatoes, taking care to slice them into similarly sized pieces to ensure everything will cook evenly when sautéed.

3 Place a large skillet over high heat, then add the oil and sauté the yellow and green onions to flavor the oil. When the yellow onions start to become translucent, add the carrots and potatoes and sauté. Add the Spam (if using). Sprinkle in the salt and stir, then add the garlic, black pepper, and chile (if you'd like some spice). Continue to sauté until the potatoes are just cooked through, 5 to 8 minutes. Carefully taste a potato. If it's still raw, sauté for 1 to 2 minutes more, then taste again—you want to avoid overcooking the potatoes. Using chopsticks or a slotted spoon, transfer everything to a serving dish. Garnish with the sesame seeds, then serve. Any leftovers can be stored in the refrigerator, covered, for 2 to 3 days.

VEGETARIAN, VEGAN (IF SPAM IS OMITTED), GLUTEN-FREE

GAMJA JORIM

감자 조림

Braised Potatoes in Soy Sauce

Serves 4

Kids and adults alike love gamja jorim. After all, who doesn't love potatoes? These are made sweet with a thin glaze of seasoned soy sauce. Because of their sweetness, they are especially good banchan to have as a counterpoint to any of the spicier dishes on the table. Here, I use red potatoes, including their nutrient-rich skins, rather than, say, russets, which aren't as flavorful and tend to lose their texture during the cooking process. The potatoes are delicious served immediately, but they will taste even better the longer they sit, as they'll absorb the liquid; expect them to turn darker in color as they do so. They will keep in an airtight container in the refrigerator for 3 or 4 days.

4   or 5 red potatoes (1½ to 2 lb / 680 to 900g), diced into ¾-inch / 2cm cubes

½   cup / 129ml Mat Ganjang / Seasoned Soy Sauce (page 88)

1   teaspoon Gahreun Mahneul / Blended Garlic (page 49)

½   teaspoon ground black pepper

1   tablespoon light corn syrup

½   teaspoon toasted sesame oil, for finishing

1   teaspoon toasted sesame seeds (page 51), for garnish

1 Place the potatoes in a large bowl and cover with cold tap water. Let soak for 15 to 20 minutes. Drain, then rinse the potatoes.

2 In a medium pot, combine the potatoes, ½ cup / 120ml water, seasoned soy sauce, garlic, and black pepper. Place over medium heat, bring to a boil, and cook until the potatoes are fork-tender, 10 to 15 minutes. Stir in the corn syrup and continue cooking until the potatoes are thoroughly coated and shiny and the liquid has reduced slightly. To finish, add the sesame oil and sprinkle with the sesame seeds. Serve.

VEGETARIAN, VEGAN

TWIGAK

튀각

Fried Sea Kelp

Serves 4

When I was a child in Korea, I often accompanied my grandmother to her Buddhist temple. There, visitors could stay for a meal made with vegetables the monks had cultivated and herbs they had foraged. The monks also picked up bundles of dashima, or sea kelp, from nearby markets; the markets sourced the dashima from Wando, an area at the southern tip of the country that was, and continues to be, famous for its seaweed. Easy to dry and easy to store, the dashima turned up in the monks' soups, rice bowls, and banchan. I was struck in particular by one way the monks prepared the kelp: after drying it, they fried it very quickly in hot oil. The fried dashima brought a delicious briny flavor and crunchy texture to many of their dishes. I remember those pieces of fried dashima to this day.

I wanted to honor the simplicity of the Buddhist traditions by incorporating fried dashima into Stone Pot Bibimbap (page 182). It's also delicious as a perfectly sweet and crispy snack, especially when served with beer. Large sheets of dashima can be found at Asian markets as well as many specialty grocers. It fries quickly, so be prepared to flip the pieces over quickly to avoid burning them.

- 2 oz / 60g dashima / dried sea kelp
- ¼ cup / 50g granulated sugar
- 1½ cups / 360ml vegetable or other neutral oil

1 Lay the dashima flat and wipe off the excess white residue with a paper towel. Tear the dashima into pieces as large or as small as you'd like.

2 Place the sugar in a small bowl next to your stove. Line a plate or baking sheet with paper towels and place next to the sugar.

3 Place a Dutch oven, large fry pan, or wok over medium heat and add the oil. Using chopsticks or tongs, tear off a small piece of dashima and drop it in the oil. If the dashima floats to the top, the oil is ready.

4 Working with just a few pieces at a time to avoid overcrowding the pan, add the dashima and fry until the pieces expand and puff up a bit, 1 or 2 seconds, then flip. If the dashima expands right when it touches the oil, the oil is too hot; adjust the heat accordingly so the dashima doesn't burn.

5 Immediately after pulling the dashima out of the frying oil, dust both sides with the sugar and lay it flat on the paper towels. Repeat with the remaining pieces.

6 To store, let cool completely, then place in an airtight container at room temperature. It will keep for up to 1 week.

VEGETARIAN, VEGAN, GLUTEN-FREE

BUCHU GEHRAN BOKKEUM

부추 계란 볶음

Grandma's Eggs and Chives

Serves 4

This side dish is inspired by my grandmother. The Korean chives used here can be found bundled at Korean and other Asian grocers, when they're in season in the spring and summer; if you can't find them, use Chinese chives instead. Because this banchan cooks in just a few minutes, have the chives and other ingredients prepped and ready to go before turning on the stove. And be sure to add the chives only when the pan is very hot. This way, the chives will soften quickly without losing their lovely green color. As they cook, keep an eye on the pan: a few seconds too long, and the chives will become tough and the eggs will overcook. You're looking for a runny texture and consistency, like loosely scrambled eggs. Serve with hot rice as a side dish to your meal.

1 tablespoon plus ½ teaspoon toasted sesame oil

2 cups / 120g sliced (about 2 inches / 5cm) Korean chives (2 to 4 bunches)

1 tablespoon Mat Ganjang / Seasoned Soy Sauce (page 88)

2 medium or large eggs

1 teaspoon toasted sesame seeds (page 51), for finishing

1 Place a small pan over high heat. Once the pan is hot, add 1 tablespoon of the sesame oil and the chives, then stir quickly for 10 seconds. Add the seasoned soy sauce and stir for about 30 seconds or until well mixed.

2 Break the eggs over the whole mixture, then turn off the heat. Stir everything gently. The eggs will cook with the residual heat. Add the sesame seeds and the remaining ½ teaspoon sesame oil to finish.

VEGETARIAN

Rolled Omelet

Serves 4

This is a popular side dish that I used to include in the lunchtime dosiraks, or bento boxes, I packed for my children when they were young. For this recipe, I add green onions, red bell peppers, and carrots to the eggs, but you can use whatever vegetables (or even imitation crabmeat or ham) you have in your fridge. For an extra kick, add minced jalapeños. And you can even add a slice of cheese or seaweed in between each egg layer if you'd like! Rolling each layer of eggs into a tight log may take a little practice to master (see photos on page 112), but I have found using chopsticks and a spatula to guide the roll is a good strategy. You can use a rectangular Korean omelet pan or Japanese tamagoyaki pan that can be found at many Asian markets as well as online. If you don't have either, a small, round nonstick frying pan works, too.

- 4 large eggs
- 2 tablespoons chopped green onions, green and white parts
- 2 tablespoons minced red bell pepper
- 1 tablespoon minced carrot
- ¼ teaspoon granulated sugar
- ¼ teaspoon sea salt, plus more to taste
- 1 tablespoon vegetable or other neutral oil

1 Beat the eggs in a small bowl with a fork. Add the green onions, bell pepper, carrot, sugar, and salt. Stir to dissolve the sugar and salt.

2 Place an omelet pan over low heat and add the oil. When the pan is hot, spoon just enough of the egg mixture to thinly cover the entire surface into the pan.

3 When the eggs have just set on the bottom but are still runny on top, use chopsticks on one end to start rolling the eggs into a log. You can use a spatula, too, to guide the egg log, as you roll it to the other side of the pan.

4 Once you've rolled the eggs to the other side, pour another thin layer of the egg mixture into the pan, lifting up the rolled egg to allow some of the raw egg mixture to spread underneath it. You want to create one continuous piece.

5 Once the eggs are just set, use the chopsticks and a spatula to roll the egg log onto the new egg layer. Continue rolling the log from one end of the pan to the other. Repeat this process with the remaining mixture, keeping the heat low as you roll.

6 When you have finished rolling up the final layer, remove the pan from the heat. Let the omelet cool for a few minutes, then transfer it to a cutting board and cut the log into slices as thick or as thin as you like. Place the slices on a serving platter to share at the table (or pack in a lunchbox!).

VEGETARIAN, GLUTEN-FREE

소세지 조림

Lunchbox Sausage

Serves 4 to 6

This is a quick and easy side dish that is both sweet and salty. Though the name of this dish (*soseji*) transliterates to "sausage" in English, it's actually hot dogs that are more typically used, and everyone loves a hot dog! It's especially great for kids; in fact, I used to make this for my daughters when they were young, tucking the hot dogs into their lunchboxes along with some steamed rice and seaweed. I use Hebrew National all-beef hot dogs, but use any brand you prefer.

- 12 oz / 340g hot dogs (about 7)
- ¼ cup plus 1 tablespoon / 75ml Mat Ganjang / Seasoned Soy Sauce (page 88)
- 1½ teaspoons Gahreun Mahneul / Blended Garlic (page 49)
- ¼ teaspoon ground black pepper
- 1 tablespoon sliced jalapeño (optional)
- 1 teaspoon toasted sesame seeds (page 51)
- 1 teaspoon toasted sesame oil

1 Cut the hot dogs diagonally into coins ¼ inch / 6mm thick. Add them to a small pot, cover with water, and turn the heat to high to bring the water to a boil. Boil the hot dogs for 5 minutes to remove some of their fat, then drain.

2 Place a medium skillet over high heat. Add the hot dogs, seasoned soy sauce, garlic, and black pepper. Stir and spoon the liquid over the hot dogs as it comes to a boil. If you like a bit of heat, add the jalapeño. Turn down the heat to medium and continue boiling until the liquid reduces to a glaze, 5 to 8 minutes. Turn off the heat and add the sesame seeds and sesame oil. Stir, then serve as part of your meal. In the unlikely chance you have leftovers, the hot dogs can be stored, covered, in the refrigerator for 3 to 4 days.

DOOBOO JORIM

두부 조림

Braised Tofu

Serves 4

This tofu is pan fried and then braised in a mix of seasoned soy sauce, gochugaru, garlic, and sesame oil. The sauce will reduce as it boils, so watch the pan and add water as necessary to maintain its consistency. If you have more than four guests or want to make enough for leftovers, use two boxes of tofu instead of just one. The leftovers can be stored in an airtight container in the fridge for three to four days. When you're ready to serve, the braised tofu is delicious served with hot steamed rice. This dish is very comforting and takes me back to my grandmother. I'm sure it'll take you back to your Korean grandmother, too—or make you wish you had one!

Sauce

- ½ cup / 120ml Mat Ganjang / Seasoned Soy Sauce (page 88)
- 2 tablespoons toasted sesame oil
- 1 tablespoon Gahreun Mahneul / Blended Garlic (page 49)
- 2 teaspoons rice cooking wine
- 1½ teaspoons coarse gochugaru
- 1½ teaspoons toasted sesame seeds (page 51)
- ¼ teaspoon ground black pepper

Tofu

- 1 tablespoon vegetable or other neutral oil
- 1 (19-oz / 538g) package medium or firm tofu, preferably House Foods brand, drained and sliced into pieces ½ inch / 12mm thick
- ½ medium yellow onion, thinly sliced
- ½ cup / 30g white beech, enoki, or button mushrooms, sliced (optional)
- 1 jalapeño or other chile pepper, sliced (optional)
- 3 tablespoons chopped green onions, green and white parts, for garnish Toasted sesame seeds (page 51), for garnish

TO MAKE THE SAUCE

Place the seasoned soy sauce, ¼ cup / 60ml water, sesame oil, garlic, cooking wine, gochugaru, sesame seeds, and black pepper in a medium bowl and mix. Set aside until ready to use.

TO COOK AND SERVE THE TOFU

1 Place a large pan over high heat and add the vegetable oil. When the oil begins to smoke, carefully add the tofu. Pan-fry until the tofu is light brown, then flip. Fry on both sides until the tofu takes on a golden hue. Pour the sauce over the tofu. Add the yellow onions, as well as the mushrooms and jalapeño (if using).

CONTINUED

2 Lower the heat to medium and spoon the sauce over the tofu and vegetables to coat. As the liquid gently boils, continue to spoon the sauce over the tofu and vegetables, adding more water as needed to maintain its consistency as the liquid evaporates.

3 After boiling for 2 to 3 minutes, turn off the heat and sprinkle the green onions and sesame seeds over the tofu. Transfer the tofu, vegetables, and braising liquid to a serving bowl or platter. As you do so, the green onions will cook slightly in the residual heat. By the time you set the tofu on the table, all the components will have come together, and it will be perfect with a bowl of rice.

VEGETARIAN, VEGAN

▶▶▶ **Potatoes or mu (Korean radishes) are a great addition to this dish.** Slice the potatoes or radishes to the same thickness as the tofu slices and set aside. Fry the tofu, then remove the pieces to a plate. In the same pan set over high heat, arrange the potatoes or radishes in a single layer. Place the fried tofu on top of the potatoes or radishes, then add the sauce, followed by the mushrooms and jalapeño (if using). Braise the potatoes or radishes in the sauce until they're fork tender, then add the green onions and sesame seeds and serve.

JANGJORIM
장조림

Braised Beef in Soy Sauce

Serves 6 to 10

Jangjorim is a nice savory side dish to complement the other dishes on your table. Back when beef was much more expensive in Korea, this banchan was a way to stretch the meat across many meals. Adding plenty of hard-boiled eggs also helped to make this banchan last. And while jangjorim is intended to be a side dish, it, like so many banchan, could also be turned into its own meal. When I was younger and didn't have much money to spend on food, I often did just that, eating leftover jangjorim with hot steamed rice and kimchi. With beef being relatively less expensive here in the United States, I tend to make jangjorim with prime-grade beef; that said, use the highest quality you can afford, and you won't be disappointed. To make the soy sauce braise, I start with garlic—a lot of it, since it not only flavors the braise but also because everyone loves fishing out a few cloves to smash into their bowls of rice. I also still add a good number of eggs, partly to stretch the banchan and partly because there's always someone who would like more than one. Once made, jangjorim will keep in an airtight container in the refrigerator for up to two weeks. In addition to serving it as banchan or with rice, the jangjorim can be added to kimchi fried rice or to any noodles you might make, where it will add an extra bit of saltiness and protein.

2 lb / 900g beef brisket, preferably prime grade, trimmed

20 garlic cloves, peeled

3 or 4 slices (to 2-inch / 2.5 to 5cm) ginger, peeled

1½ cups / 360ml soy sauce

1 cup / 240ml rice cooking wine

½ cup / 100g granulated sugar

1 jalapeño, seeded and sliced into ¼-inch / 6mm pieces

10 small or medium hard-boiled eggs

1 Cut the brisket into 2 by 2-inch / 5 by 5cm pieces and soak in cold tap water for 1 hour.

2 Place a large pot over high heat, add 10 cups / 2.4L water, and bring to a boil. Add the brisket and boil for 10 to 15 minutes, then use a slotted spoon to skim off the fat and scum that float to the surface. Continue to boil for 40 minutes more, then poke the center of a brisket piece with a sharp knife. If the juices still run red, continue to boil until they are clear, 5 to 10 more minutes. Add the garlic, ginger, soy sauce, cooking wine, sugar, and jalapeño.

3 Turn down the heat to medium and continue to cook for another 30 to 45 minutes, then discard the ginger and use tongs to remove the brisket to a bowl. Cool for 10 minutes. Hand-shred the brisket into bite-sized pieces, then place the pieces back into the pot along with the eggs. Boil on medium until the brisket is tender, 10 to 15 minutes.

4 Turn off the heat and serve with other dishes or with hot steamed rice. To store leftovers, cool the brisket to room temperature, then place the meat and its liquid in an airtight container and refrigerate. It will keep for 5 to 7 days.

While hard-boiled eggs are usually served with jangjorim, you can also fry the eggs if you prefer. To serve, place a fried egg and some beef on top of hot steamed rice, spoon plenty of braising liquid over the bowl, and finish with a dash of toasted sesame oil and a sprinkling of your favorite furikake seasoning.

EOMUK JORIM
어묵 조림

Soy-Braised Fish Cakes

Serves 4 to 6

This is a great chewy, salty, and spicy banchan to add to the table. Fish cakes are the main ingredient here, making this a tasty option for those who would prefer not to have any beef or pork (in fact, when my children were young, I liked to pack this banchan into their lunches so they weren't always eating meat). These fish cakes are best enjoyed the day they're made, or soon after; I don't recommend keeping them in the refrigerator for very long, because the texture will harden. If you do need to reheat them, you can try to re-create the original texture by adding a little water and adjusting the soy sauce to taste. My preferred brand of fish cake is Sempio, which is available at Korean grocers.

- 12 oz / 340g fish cakes
- ½ cup / 120ml Mat Ganjang / Seasoned Soy Sauce (page 88)
- 1 tablespoon Maeun Yangnum / Spicy Red Pepper Marinade (page 88)
- 1 tablespoon Gahreun Mahneul / Blended Garlic (page 49)
- ½ teaspoon ground black pepper
- ½ medium yellow onion, diced
- ½ bell pepper (any color), diced
- ½ jalapeño, seeds removed, thinly sliced (optional)
- 2 green onions, green parts only, sliced into 1-inch / 2.5cm pieces
- 1 teaspoon toasted sesame oil
- 1½ teaspoons toasted sesame seeds (page 51), for garnish

1 Bring a large pot of water to a boil over high heat. Drop the fish cakes into the water for 30 seconds to remove the excess oil, then drain and let cool. Slice the fish cakes into 1½-inch / 4cm square pieces and return to the pot. Add the seasoned soy sauce, red pepper marinade, garlic, black pepper, and ½ cup / 120ml water, stir, then turn the heat to high. As the mixture comes to a boil, spoon the liquid over the fish cakes to thoroughly flavor the fish. The fish cakes will release some residual starch and thicken the sauce, and the sauce will reduce as it continues to boil.

2 When the fish cakes are tender, 2 to 3 minutes, stir in the yellow onions, bell peppers, and jalapeño (if using). Keep stirring until the vegetables are cooked to al dente, 5 to 8 minutes. Add the green onions and sesame oil and mix well. Transfer the fish cakes to a small serving dish or bowl—or into a lunchbox!—and finish with a garnish of sesame seeds.

121

Kimchi

No Korean meal is complete without kimchi. Because it is always on the table and so widely available at supermarkets, I think sometimes we underappreciate the care and time that goes into making it. Homemade kimchi is fresh, light, and crisp, and, unlike store-bought kimchi, can be customized with the best ingredients. Store-bought kimchi also is a bit unpredictable, not only because you don't know the quality of the ingredients but also because it is difficult to gauge how long the kimchi has been sitting (and fermenting) on the shelf. Often, by the time you take it home, the kimchi is nearly past its peak ripeness, and you don't have much of a window to enjoy it before it sours. When you make your own kimchi, you can decide when it's ripe enough to have with your meal.

Most of the kimchi recipes in this section are made using the same process. First, the vegetables are carefully cleaned. Then, the kimchi paste (or brine) is prepared and mixed together. Finally, the vegetables are coated with the paste. It is quite a bit of work, but do not let that deter you! It is rewarding. By the end of it, you will have delicious kimchi for weeks, if not months, to come.

It does help to have family and friends pitch in. In fact, making kimchi has long been a communal activity. In the Korea of my great-grandmother and grandmother's time, access to fresh vegetables was very limited during the winter, so it was necessary to make enough kimchi to last until the early spring. Before the onset of the cold weather, families, friends, and neighbors gathered for kimjang, an annual ritual where everyone cleaned and trimmed hundreds of pounds of vegetables to make kimchi. The vegetables were packed into large earthenware jars and buried underground, where they fermented and fed families for months.

Things are very different now, at least in the United States. Fresh vegetables are available at supermarkets year round, and not only do we have refrigerators to store them and other perishables, there are also refrigerators specifically made to store kimchi!

Those kimchi refrigerators, with their precise temperature controls, are very nice to have, but you do not need one to make kimchi. So long as you properly store the kimchi in an airtight container and keep an eye on it, fermenting your kimchi on your countertop or in your kitchen refrigerator is just fine. Generally, you can make kimchi out of any vegetable, but I highly recommend using vegetables that are in season, when they are at their most vibrant and flavorful (see below).

KIMCHI BY THE SEASON

Most of my kimchi can be made any time of the year, but they will taste best if you use the vegetables that are in season. If you would like to prepare my kimchi according to the season, use this chart to guide you.

SEASON	KIMCHI
Late fall/early winter	Mak Kimchi (page 129)
	Tongbaechoo Kimchi / Spicy Napa Cabbage Kimchi (page 130)
	Baek Kimchi / Non-Spicy White Napa Cabbage Kimchi (page 139)
	Chonggak Kimchi / Ponytail Radish Kimchi (page 142)
Late winter/spring	Kkakdoogi Kimchi / Radish Kimchi (page 141): Look for delicious radishes from Jeju Island at your local Korean market.
Spring	Pa Kimchi / Green Onion Kimchi (page 145)
Summer	Pootbaechoo Kimchi / Young Cabbage Kimchi (page 146)
	Bok Choy Kimchi (page 148)
Year-round	Oh Eeh Kimchi / Cucumber Kimchi (page 151)
	Yangpa Kimchi / Yellow Onion Kimchi (page 152)
	Yang Baechoo Kimchi / Green Cabbage Kimchi (page 158)

Most of my recipes for the kimchi paste include gochugaru for spice, and all include salted shrimp. I recommend using quality gochugaru from a reputable brand; high-quality gochugaru will be bright red in color, will keep your vegetables crisper for longer, and its peppery notes will shine through (for more on shopping for gochugaru, see page 23). Lesser-quality or stale pepper flakes, in contrast, are duller in color, will quickly soften the vegetables, and will mute the flavor of your kimchi. The salted shrimp adds flavor and aids in the fermentation process. Salted shrimp can be overly salty, so I blend it with a little bit of water before working with it. As I explain on page 25, blending also makes it easier to distribute the shrimp evenly throughout the kimchi mixture.

Once you have prepared the vegetables, it's time to pack them into a clean, nonreactive container to ferment. Glass mason jars are popular choices, as are containers made with food-grade plastic. Many Korean cookware shops and online sources sell plastic and stainless-steel containers specifically intended for fermenting kimchi. Those containers come in square and rectangular shapes, making them convenient for storage. You can also ferment the kimchi in double-bagged resealable freezer bags; because you can lay them flat, these are excellent options if you don't have much space in your kitchen or refrigerator. If you make my kimchi often, it's handy to have several 1- to 3-qt / 1 to 2.8L containers on hand, since that is how much kimchi most of my recipes make. As you pack the vegetables into the container, be sure to completely submerge the vegetables in the liquid and leave about 1 inch / 2.5cm of headroom so they have room to expand while they ferment.

Once the vegetables are packed, bacteria will do its work to ferment them. As a result of that fermentation process, the vegetables will ripen. The time it takes for the vegetables to ferment and ripen to a point where they taste rich and sweetly sour with a pleasant, gentle acidity, while maintaining a bit of crispness, may take anywhere from a few days to a few weeks, which is why it is very important to taste your kimchi often. My recipes note how long a kimchi may take to ripen, and how long it may stay ripe before it sours, but these are very rough guidelines. The fermentation process very much depends on the temperature of your environment. Left on a countertop, the kimchi will ferment much faster in the summer than in the winter. Once in the cold of a refrigerator, fermentation will slow down, but how much it slows down will depend on the temperature of your refrigerator and even on how often you open and close your refrigerator throughout the day.

Taste your kimchi every morning and you will discover how the flavor changes from one day to the next. Make kimchi often enough, and you will be able to predict the time it will take for your kimchi to ripen to your desired flavor and texture.

Even if you don't taste your kimchi every day, it is a good idea to open the container when you notice bubbles in the liquid. These bubbles are gases produced during the fermentation process; if not released, the gases will build up in your container and cause your container to burst from the pressure.

I use ripened kimchi for many things: as part of an array of banchan in a meal, as an ingredient in dishes like my Tofu Steak with Kimchi (page 169) and Stone Pot Bibimbap with Tofu and Kimchi (page 186), and on its own as a snack. Because of its versatility, it is difficult to estimate how many people a kimchi recipe will serve. For that reason, each recipe here indicates how much kimchi you will make rather than a specific serving size.

Given how much effort is involved in making kimchi and the fact that it goes well with everything, I tend to make big batches. I make enough so I can have at least one jar out on my counter to eat right away. A few go into my refrigerator to ripen more slowly, and any remaining ones I gift to family and friends.

As your kimchi ages, the vegetables will release water. This water will separate from the rest of the brine and collect at the bottom of the container. Before eating or using the kimchi, I recommend recombining the water with the brine so the wonderful flavor of the kimchi seasoning is evenly distributed. To do so, first make sure the lid is tightly closed, then carefully invert the container a few times to remix the brine.

At some point, though, your kimchi will overripen and be too fermented and sour to eat on its own. But even at this stage, the kimchi still has its uses: it is perfect in a stew or as part of a stir-fry. Unless there is mold on the kimchi (often as a result of improper storage), no kimchi is thrown out or discarded in my house. With the amount of work and care that goes into making it, kimchi is too precious to waste. Homemade kimchi is a labor of love. Once you make it, I'm sure you will feel the same way.

WHAT TO DO WITH OVERRIPENED KIMCHI

When your kimchi becomes too ripe, it will taste sour and overly fermented, but that is not a reason to throw it out—the opposite is true! That is even more reason to use it. Below are recipe suggestions for the many different ways you can use your very ripe kimchi.

· Gogi Kimchi Soon Tofu / Beef or Pork Kimchi Soon Tofu (page 60)

· Kimchi Dooboo Steak / Tofu Steak with Kimchi (page 169)

· Kimchi Chigae / Kimchi Stew (page 223)

· Kimchi Jeon / Kimchi Pancakes (page 164)

· Nokdoo Bindaedduk / Mung Bean Pancakes (page 160)

· Kimchi Guk / Kimchi Soup (page 226)

· Kimchi Bokkeumbap / Kimchi Fried Rice (page 179)

갈은 새우젓

Blended Salted Shrimp

Makes ¾ cup / 250g

Tiny shrimp that have been salted and fermented are the base for most of my kimchi recipes. Right out of the jar, the salted shrimp are quite salty—sometimes, depending on the needs of a dish, a little *too* salty. To dilute it, I blend the shrimp with a bit of water, making large batches at a time so they are ready to use anytime I need them. The flavor of the shrimp itself won't be diluted; rather, its briny flavor will come through even more and will better complement many Korean dishes. Note that some brands are saltier than others, so you may need to taste and blend in more water if needed. This recipe will make enough for my Spicy Napa Cabbage Kimchi (page 130), with a small amount left over that will keep well for up to six months and can be used to make other kimchi. If you're working with a recipe that needs just a few tablespoons, you can make this mixture using a ratio of 1 part shrimp to ½ part water (that is, blend 1 tablespoon of salted shrimp with 1½ teaspoons of water) and adjust the taste from there.

½ cup (2¼ oz / 60g) salted shrimp

In a blender, combine ¼ cup / 60ml water and the salted shrimp. Blend until combined. The mixture will be watery but will still have some body. Place leftovers in an airtight container and refrigerate. It will easily keep in your refrigerator for 6 months.

막김치

Mak Kimchi

Makes about 1 qt / 960g

The most common kimchi you see in restaurants and supermarkets is a spicy kimchi made with napa cabbage. Traditionally, family and friends came together to make the kimchi from pounds and pounds of napa cabbage, brining the heads for several hours before carefully layering the kimchi marinade onto each and every cabbage leaf (see page 130). The result is a kimchi full of depth and flavor. But it takes quite a bit of time to prepare, and since it's intended to be shared, it yields quite a large quantity. For a more everyday alternative, make mak kimchi.

Mak literally translates to "without thinking," though this direct translation is a little harsher than what it implies. It's not that making mak kimchi is mindless or thoughtless. Rather, it is so quick and simple to make, you can make it almost instinctively. Here the cabbage leaves are sliced into bite-sized pieces before being brined for just ten minutes. Then they're tossed in the marinade with chives. (Korean chives are ideal when their leaves are at least ¼ inch / 6mm thick, usually when they're in season in the spring and summer. Otherwise, Chinese chives will do just fine.) It can be eaten as soon as it's made, though I like to leave it out to ferment overnight during the warmer summer months and a little longer in colder weather to develop the flavors a bit. The short brining and fermentation periods ensure you get the taste of the kimchi but with minimal effort and time.

1	lb / 450g napa cabbage (about ¼ medium head), sliced into 1½- to 2-inch / 4 to 5cm square pieces
1½	teaspoons sea salt
½	cup / 60g thinly sliced medium yellow onions
½	cup / 115g sliced (1½ to 2 inches / 4 to 5cm) green onions, green and white parts
½	cup / 30g sliced (1½ to 2 inches / 4 to 5cm) Korean or Chinese chives (about ½ bunch)
2½	tablespoons coarse gochugaru
4½	teaspoons granulated sugar
1	tablespoon Gahreun Mahneul / Blended Garlic (page 49)
1½	teaspoons Gahreun Saeoo Jut / Blended Salted Shrimp (opposite)
1½	teaspoons fish sauce
½	teaspoon Gahreun Senggang / Blended Ginger (page 89)

1 Add the cabbage to a large bowl and sprinkle the salt all over the cabbage. Set aside for 10 minutes. Add the yellow onions, green onions, and chives and mix together.

2 In a small bowl, mix together the gochugaru, garlic, sugar, salted shrimp, fish sauce, ginger, and ½ cup / 120ml water. Add the wet ingredients into the bowl with the cabbage and other vegetables and mix until well incorporated.

3 The kimchi can be eaten immediately if you like the flavor. Otherwise, cover the bowl and leave it overnight on your counter. The next morning, mix everything again from bottom to top and taste. If you like the flavor, it's ready to eat; if not, let it ferment for a few more hours. When you're happy with the taste, transfer the kimchi to an airtight 1-qt / 600g glass jar or other food-grade container and refrigerate.

TONGBAECHOO KIMCHI
통배추 김치

Spicy Napa Cabbage Kimchi

Makes 2 to 3 gal / 5.5-8.25kg

When I was a child in Korea, the beginning of winter meant it was time to make this kimchi. Access to fresh vegetables was very limited during the winter months, so kimchi was the main vegetable on our table until the spring. Preparing the kimchi was a communal event called kimjang, and during kimjang, families and friends gathered and worked together to turn hundreds of pounds of napa cabbage into kimchi. Though times have changed, the ritual still holds cultural significance today; when the children were young, our family would come together to make this kimchi as part of our own kimjang. Everyone went home with jars of kimchi for themselves and to gift to their friends. Though my children are now adults, I still like to make this kimchi in the late fall and early winter, when the cabbage is in season and at its peak flavor. Of course, because napa cabbage is plentiful year-round here in the United States, you can make this kimchi anytime you wish. When shopping, look for heads that are heavy for their size, with creamy white stalks and tightly packed, light green leaves. For the chives, which one to use will depend on the season; I use Korean chives when they are at their best in the spring and summer, and Chinese chives all other times of the year.

To ferment and store the kimchi, I typically use a 1-gallon / 3.8L jar, container, or resealable freezer bag for each head of cabbage. If you do not have much refrigerator space, I recommend resealable bags, since they can be laid flat on the shelf. Be sure to double-bag the kimchi to prevent spillage. Alternatively, the cabbage can be divided among several 1-quart / 1L containers, which may be easier to store and distribute to loved ones.

Making all kimchi is a labor of love, but this one, with its tradition rooted in community and familial bonding, is even more so. Even just the act of making this kimchi connects you with your loved ones. Rather than simply slicing the cabbage leaves with your knife, as you do with Mak Kimchi (page 129), here you tear the whole head lengthwise into quarters so the leaves stay intact. You also use your hands to salt the cabbage before brining and then again to slather the kimchi paste directly onto each and every cabbage leaf, layer by layer.

In the spirit of kimjang, I encourage you to invite your family and friends over to make this kimchi together. It certainly will yield enough for everyone to take home as much as they'd like, and you and your loved ones will be able to appreciate the time and care that went into making this kimchi.

10 lb / 4.5kg napa cabbage (2 to 3 napa cabbage heads)

¾ cup plus 1 tablespoon / 215g sea salt

¼ lb / 113g Chinese chives, cut into 2-inch / 5cm pieces (1 or 2 bunches)

½ medium yellow onion, thinly sliced

½ bunch red mustard leaves, cut into 2-inch / 5cm pieces

½ bunch green onions (4 or 5 green onions), green and white parts, sliced into 2-inch / 5cm pieces

2½ cups / 450g coarse gochugaru

½ cup / 125g Gahreun Mahneul / Blended Garlic (page 49)

½ cup / 167g Gahreun Saeoo Jut / Blended Salted Shrimp (page 128)

½ cup / 120ml fish sauce

½ cup / 100g granulated sugar

1½ teaspoons Gahreun Senggang / Blended Ginger (page 89)

1 Trim the wilted or tough outer leaves of the cabbage and discard. Working with one head at a time, slice just the white base in half. Place your thumbs in the cut section and tear the cabbage cleanly in half. Cut the white base of each piece of the torn cabbage in half again, then tear again so you end up with four hand-torn pieces. Repeat with the remaining heads.

2 Place ¾ cup / 178g of the salt in a bowl. Take a handful of the salt and sprinkle it along the

surface of each leaf of a quartered cabbage, being extra generous around the thick stems. Repeat for all the cabbage. I am careful with the amount of salt here; the cabbage will lose its crispness as more salt is added. In addition, the kimchi marinade contains fish sauce and salted shrimp, both salty ingredients. Since it's much easier to add than to remove salt, it is a good idea to be prudent with the salt at this early stage.

3 Place the quartered sections side by side in one or more large containers with tall sides. You can use what you have on hand, like a deep baking or casserole dish, a large basin, or a dishpan, or you can even stack the cabbage if necessary. Pour enough cold tap water into the container so three-quarters of the cabbage is submerged, then place a heavy weight (a clean plate with a few cans of food will work) on top. Let the cabbage sit for about 2 hours, then, if you've stacked your cabbage, rotate the heads so the bottom is now on top, allowing each piece to be evenly brined in the salt water. Replace the heavy weight and set aside for another 2 hours. After brining, the cabbage will be wilted but the leaves should still have some crunch to them.

CONTINUED

4 Drain and rinse the quartered cabbage pieces in cold tap water. If necessary, carefully trim any darkly yellowed ends of the leaves so the pieces are similarly sized, then place the cabbage side by side in a single layer in large colanders and set aside to drain.

5 To make the paste, in a large bowl, combine 5 cups / 1.2L water with the chives, yellow onions, red mustard leaves, green onions, gochugaru, garlic, salted shrimp, fish sauce, sugar, the remaining 1 tablespoon salt, and the ginger. Mix well. You should have enough kimchi paste for all the cabbage, but when you are first making kimchi, I suggest dividing the paste into as many portions as you have heads of cabbage to ensure you will have enough paste for all the cabbage.

6 Put on your gloves. Take one of the quartered cabbage pieces in your hand, with the cut side facing up. With your other hand, scoop up some of the kimchi paste and carefully spread the paste on the surface of each leaf, giving the white, firmer sections around the stalk a slightly thicker coat than the thinner, more delicate green tops. Carefully place the cabbage, cut side up, into a 1-gallon / 3.8L container.

CONTINUED

7 As you fit each quartered section into the container, pack them tightly but not too tightly: they will need a little bit of room to expand as they ferment. Each 1-gallon / 3.8L container should fit 4 quartered pieces (or one whole head) of cabbage.

8 When you're done, distribute the kimchi among your friends and family. If you end up with several containers of kimchi, I suggest managing the fermentation process by placing all but one in the fridge. The refrigerated containers will ripen and ferment slowly over the next few weeks. The container you leave at room temperature will ripen and be ready to eat more quickly. Set it on your counter, covered, for at least one night. If you'd like to accelerate the fermentation process even more, leave it out for another night, then place the kimchi in the refrigerator. It will continue to ferment in the fridge, but because it had a head start on the fermentation process, it will reach its peak ripeness faster than the containers you immediately refrigerated. Taste the kimchi every morning until it is as crisp and ripe as you'd like, then enjoy with your meals.

GLUTEN-FREE IF USING GLUTEN-FREE FISH SAUCE

Non-Spicy White Napa Cabbage Kimchi

Makes 2 qt / 1.92kg

This kimchi is made with napa cabbage, and while it is flavored with slices of jalapeño, it's not spicy at all. Chives add flavor to the kimchi; I use Korean chives when their leaves are thick (about ¼ inch / 6mm). If the only ones you can find are thin and stringy, Chinese chives are an excellent alternative. The kimchi will be ready to serve the day after preparing it, but for a richer, more fermented, and slightly more sour taste, transfer the kimchi to an airtight container and leave it on your counter to ferment for another day or two before serving. It can be stored, covered, in your fridge.

2 to 3 lb / 900g to 1.4kg napa cabbage (about ½ medium head), cored and cut into 1½- to 2-inch / 4 to 5cm slices

3 tablespoons granulated sugar

2 tablespoons Gahreun Mahneul / Blended Garlic (page 49)

1 tablespoon sea salt

1 tablespoon fish sauce

1 tablespoon Gahreun Saeoo Jut / Blended Salted Shrimp (page 128)

1 teaspoon Gahreun Senggang / Blended Ginger (page 89)

1 jalapeño, seeded

½ red bell pepper

½ medium yellow onion

½ bunch Korean or Chinese chives

2 or 3 green onions

1 Place the cabbage in a large bowl, add 2 cups / 480ml cold tap water, salt, fish sauce, salted shrimp, the sugar, garlic, and ginger, and mix.

2 Cut the jalapeño, bell pepper, and yellow onion into slices the same thickness as the cabbage. (You should end up with about ½ cup / 75g bell pepper and ½ cup / 60g yellow onion.) Add them to the bowl with the cabbage.

3 Slice the chives and green onions into pieces 1½ to 2 inches / 4 to 5cm long; you should have about ¼ cup / 20g of each. Place the chives and green onions into the bowl with the cabbage, then mix thoroughly.

4 Transfer the entire mixture to a 2-qt / 2L glass jar or other food-grade container with a lid and set aside at room temperature, covered, overnight. The following morning, place the kimchi in the fridge and serve cold.

5 Alternatively, transfer the kimchi to an airtight food-grade container and leave at room temperature for one day, then taste it. If it's to your liking, place the kimchi in the fridge. If you'd like an even more fermented flavor, leave it out for one more day, then place it in the fridge. In either case, the kimchi is best eaten within 2 weeks. After that point, it may start to sour.

GLUTEN-FREE IF USING GLUTEN-FREE FISH SAUCE

MIXING BY HAND

I mix many ingredients for my dishes with my hands, and that is especially true when I make kimchi. I strongly recommend you do the same. Through your hands, you can feel whether the ingredients in the kimchi paste are thoroughly combined or if it needs a little more mixing. Applying the kimchi paste onto the vegetables with your hands is messier than using a spoon or other utensil, but you will be able to ensure that every part of the vegetable—every leaf, every corner—is evenly coated. And for delicate vegetables like ponytail radishes that require careful handling, a utensil may actually break or bruise the leaves.

To avoid staining your clothes and hands, wear an apron and gloves. You may sometimes need to feel the paste with your bare hands to judge whether it's been fully mixed or not, so having multiple pairs of gloves will be handy. Any pair of gloves will do. Korean markets sell rubber gloves in a range of thicknesses and lengths, from those that cover your wrists to others that go all the way up your arm. These are perfect for making kimchi.

Even after following my recipes, I'm sure your kimchi will taste different from mine. Every kitchen has different temperatures that will affect how the kimchi ferments. Every family has their own preferred amount of saltiness and spice. And every cook has a different level of experience. The more you practice making kimchi, and cooking in general, the better your results will be.

Beyond your environment, there is also another, more intangible factor that affects how your kimchi tastes, and it goes back to your hands. Every pair of hands brings a different flavor to a dish. Your intentions, your thoughts, your feelings all flow from your hands into the kimchi, or for that matter, any other dish you're making. If your sohn-mat is strong, your hands will instinctively know exactly what seasoning and adjustments need to be made to bring out all the delicious flavors. I truly believe you, your family, and your loved ones can taste your intentions and your sohn-mat. Like a fingerprint or a signature, the flavors of your hands are what make your dishes uniquely your own.

Radish Kimchi

Makes 2 qt / 1.8kg

Mu (Korean radishes) are firm, crisp, and have a nice peppery bite. For all these reasons, they make excellent kimchi. These stout radishes can be found at Asian markets year round, but how crisp and juicy they are will depend on the season. Late winter, around January and February, is a good time for the radish, but my favorite radishes come in the spring, when radishes shipped from Jeju Island arrive at our local Korean markets. These radishes have a very short window of availability, but since they are grown in the island's rich volcanic soil, they are absolutely delicious. Regardless of the time of year, look for radishes that are firm and smooth with a creamy white skin. This kimchi can be eaten the day after making it, but if you prefer more prominent sour notes, leave it out at room temperature until you see bubbles in the liquid, then give it a try.

- 3 **lb / 900g mu (Korean radishes) (2 to 3 medium radishes)**
- 1 **tablespoon sea salt, plus more to taste**
- 4 **tablespoons plus 1½ teaspoons / 64g granulated sugar, plus more to taste**
- ¼ **cup plus 2 tablespoons / 67g coarse gochugaru, plus more to taste**
- 2 **tablespoons Gahreun Mahneul / Blended Garlic (page 49)**
- 2 **tablespoons fish sauce**
- 2 **tablespoons Gahreun Saeoo Jut / Blended Salted Shrimp (page 128)**
- 1 **teaspoon Gahreun Senggang / Blended Ginger (page 89)**

1 If the skin of the radishes is especially thick and fibrous, peel and discard. Cube the radishes into ¾-inch / 2cm pieces and place in a large bowl. Sprinkle the salt and 1½ teaspoons of the sugar over the radishes and set aside for 30 to 45 minutes. During this time, the radishes will release some of their water. Do not discard the liquid; you will use it in the next step.

2 In another large bowl, mix together the gochugaru, the remaining 4 tablespoons / 50g sugar, the garlic, fish sauce, salted shrimp, and ginger. Add the radishes with their liquid and mix. Taste and adjust, adding up to 1 tablespoon more sugar or additional salt or gochugaru to taste.

3 Place the radish mixture in a 2-qt / 2L glass jar or other container. The liquid should cover the radishes completely. Cover the container and set aside. The kimchi is ready to eat the following morning. If you prefer, continue to ferment the kimchi until you see bubbles in the liquid, about 1 day in warm weather. At that point, mix the radishes from the bottom of the jar to the top, then place in an airtight glass or plastic food-grade container and refrigerate. It will keep for up to 1 month before it begins to sour.

GLUTEN-FREE IF USING GLUTEN-FREE FISH SAUCE

CHONGGAK KIMCHI

총각 김치

Ponytail Radish Kimchi

Makes about 4 qt / 2.6kg

Chonggak radishes have nicknames that take you back to the very old days of Korea. Back then, hair signified marital status. Young unmarried men wore their hair in long ponytails until they wed. When they married, they bundled their hair at the top of their head, which was then often covered by a hat. It is said that the stems of the radish resemble the hair of the unmarried men during that time, and it's because of this resemblance that these radishes are often called ponytail radishes or bachelor radishes.

Ponytail radishes can be found at Korean and some Asian markets year round, but they are at their best when they are in season in the late fall. This is my favorite kimchi to eat in the winter, because it has such a wonderful contrast of textures. Even after fermenting, the radishes and their stems retain their mild, refreshing crunch, while the leaves are softer and more delicate. It's a nice break from the napa cabbage kimchi that we typically have on the table. This kimchi is also special because of the work involved in making it. When purchased, the radishes are usually still covered in soil and require some time to clean. And once brined, they must be handled gently, ideally one by one, or else they will lose their shape, and their leaves will tear. Because it requires such care to make, you rarely see this kimchi in restaurants. Still, it is worth making and adding to your kimchi repertoire, especially for special occasions.

6	lb / 2.7kg ponytail radishes (about 12 bunches or 30 to 36 radishes)
5	tablespoons / 80g sea salt
1	medium yellow onion, thinly sliced
1½	cups / 270g coarse gochugaru
¾	cup / 150g granulated sugar
½	cup / 125g Gahreun Mahneul / Blended Garlic (page 49)
⅓	cup / 111g Gahreun Saeoo Jut / Blended Salted Shrimp (page 128)
⅓	cup / 80ml fish sauce
1½	teaspoons Gahreun Senggang / Blended Ginger (page 89)
4	bunches green onions, root ends trimmed (select the thinnest bunches you can find)

1 Use a knife or a peeler to scrape and clean the surface of the radishes, then carefully use your knife to trim away any dirt that may have collected around the stems. Discard any leaves that are tough or discolored.

2 Carefully lay the trimmed radishes side by side next to your sink. One by one, wash the radishes five or six times or until they are thoroughly cleaned. After washing, place them in a colander to drain.

3 Line up the washed radishes neatly in a large square or rectangular glass or food-grade container at least 4 qt / 3.8L in volume, like a 10 by 14-inch / 25 by 36cm baking or casserole dish, keeping the root ends together. Sprinkle 3 tablespoons of the salt over the radishes, taking care to dust each radish with a more generous shower on the thicker tops.

4 After salting, pour enough cold tap water into the container to submerge about three-quarters

CONTINUED

of the radishes. Cover with plastic wrap, applying the film directly onto the radishes. Place a heavy weight, like a pot filled with water, on top. Let sit for 45 minutes. Flip the radishes over and replace the plastic wrap and the weight and set aside for another 45 minutes. Rinse the radishes in cold water and place in a colander to drain.

5 While the radishes drain, rinse out the container. Pour 2 cups / 480ml water into the container and add the yellow onions, gochugaru, sugar, garlic, salted shrimp, fish sauce, the remaining 2 tablespoons salt, and the ginger. Mix well. Add the whole green onions and coat them with the mixture, then move all the onions to one side of the container.

6 Take one radish in one hand and a handful of the kimchi paste in the other. Coat the entire radish, including its stem and leaves, with an even layer of the paste. Be gentle as

you do so since the radish may lose its shape if handled too roughly; its stem and leaves are delicate and will tear easily. Place the radish to the side next to the onions. Scoop up more of the kimchi paste and coat the remaining radishes. When all the radishes are coated, gently mix the onions together with the radishes; the onions should be dispersed throughout. Arrange the coated radishes side by side in a single layer in the container, then reverse the direction of the radishes as you stack them to form a second layer.

7 Most or all of the radishes should be submerged in the liquid. Cover and refrigerate. Personally, I like to let the kimchi ferment for a few days before eating, but taste the radishes daily until they are ripened to your liking. Stored in an airtight container, this kimchi will keep for up to 2 months before it begins to sour.

GLUTEN-FREE IF USING GLUTEN-FREE FISH SAUCE

Green Onion Kimchi

Makes about 1 qt / 750g

I make this kimchi throughout the year, but it is the very best when made during the spring, when green onions are in season and are at their most tender and flavorful. When shopping, look for bunches with the thinnest stalks. Korean markets usually have a wide variety of green onions no matter the season. The green onions are beautiful when presented whole, so I keep the bunches uncut as I prepare them. To serve, bring the whole platter to the table and use scissors to cut the onions into halves or thirds. Or, if you have some time, you can be creative with how you present the onions. For special occasions, I like to take a few green onions and wrap one of them around the bunch to form knotted bundles.

6	to 8 bunches green onions, root ends trimmed
1	teaspoon fish sauce
1	teaspoon Gahreun Saeoo Jut / Blended Salted Shrimp (page 128)
¼	cup / 45g coarse gochugaru
1½	teaspoons Gahreun Mahneul / Blended Garlic (page 49)
1	teaspoon sea salt
1	teaspoon granulated sugar
¼	teaspoon Gahreun Senggang / Blended Ginger (page 89)

1 Wash each onion thoroughly, one by one, until all the dirt has been removed. Shake off the excess water.

2 Place the onions flat in a 9 by 13-inch / 24 by 36cm glass baking dish or similarly sized food-grade container with a lid, keeping the root ends together so each bunch is layered in the same direction. If you don't have a rectangular container with a lid, you can cover it tightly with plastic wrap. I suggest multiple layers of plastic wrap, or else your refrigerator may end up smelling a bit like kimchi for a few days! If you don't have a rectangular container, you can coil the green onions in a 1-qt / 1L glass jar instead. Spoon the fish sauce and salted shrimp over the green onions, pouring a little more heavily over the thicker white parts. Set aside for 10 minutes.

3 In a medium bowl, combine ¼ cup / 60ml water with the gochugaru, garlic, salt, sugar, and ginger and pour over the green onions. Use your hands to mix the green onions with the mixture, then place the lid on the container and set aside overnight. Taste the kimchi every day until it's ripened to your preference, then refrigerate. After refrigeration, it will stay ripe for about 2 weeks; after that, it may begin to overripen and sour.

GLUTEN-FREE IF USING GLUTEN-FREE FISH SAUCE

SPINOFF

With just a few additional ingredients, you can turn this kimchi into a banchan that is as good with Korean BBQ as it is with a simple bowl of hot steamed white rice. Take 4 to 6 green onions from the kimchi, chop them into 1-inch / 2.5cm pieces, and combine them with ½ teaspoon toasted sesame oil, ½ teaspoon granulated sugar, and ½ teaspoon toasted sesame seeds (page 51). Mix well and your banchan is ready to serve.

POOTBAECHOO KIMCHI

풋배추 김치

Young Cabbage Kimchi

Makes about 2 qt / 1.8kg

This kimchi is best made in the summer, when young (sometimes called "baby") napa cabbage is in season and plentiful at Asian markets. Much thinner, smaller, and more tender than the full-sized variety of napa cabbage, young cabbage is sold in bunches. When shopping, look for heads that are 4 to 5 inches / 10 to 13cm in length, with crisp leaves that snap cleanly when broken. Once it's made, you can serve this kimchi right away or set it out for a day or two to ripen. Either way, it will be light and refreshing and taste just like summer.

- 3   lb / 1.4kg young napa cabbage (about 6 bunches)
- 1   tablespoon plus ½ teaspoon sea salt
- ½   cup / 30g sliced (about 2 inches / 5cm) Korean or Chinese chives (½ bunch)
- ½   cup / 60g thinly sliced yellow onions
- ¼   cup / 40g thinly sliced red bell peppers (about 3 mini bell peppers)
- 2   green onions, green and white parts, thinly sliced
- ¼   cup plus 1 tablespoon / 56g coarse gochugaru
- 2½   tablespoons Gahreun Saeoo Jut / Blended Salted Shrimp (page 128)
- 2½   tablespoons fish sauce
- 2   tablespoons Gahreun Mahneul / Blended Garlic (page 49)
- 2   tablespoons granulated sugar
- 1   teaspoon Gahreun Senggang / Blended Ginger (page 89)

1 Trim away any tough outer pieces of the young cabbages and reserve for soup (see Spinoff). Wash the trimmed cabbages in brisk running water to remove any dirt.

2 Place the cabbages in a large bowl. Sprinkle 1 tablespoon of the salt over the cabbages and pour in 1 cup / 240 ml cold tap water. Place a small plate or other flat heavy object on top of the cabbages to weigh down the heads so they are completely submerged. Set aside for 30 to 40 minutes.

3 Remove the cabbages and discard the water and any residual dirt. Rinse the cabbages again with cold water. You'll notice that at this point the cabbages will have reduced to about half their original size, due to the salt drawing out their moisture. After rinsing, shake the cabbages a few times to remove the excess water, but do not worry about completely drying the heads: any remaining liquid will be mixed with the other ingredients. Place in a colander and set aside.

4 Add the chives, yellow onions, bell peppers, and green onions to the bowl. Add 1 cup / 240ml water, the gochugaru, salted shrimp, fish sauce, garlic, sugar, ginger, and remaining ½ teaspoon salt and mix well. Add the rinsed cabbage and mix just until all the marinade has been incorporated into the cabbage; do not overmix.

5 After mixing, the kimchi can be eaten immediately. Alternatively, transfer the vegetables to a 2-qt / 2L glass jar or other food-grade container and cover. Set the jar on your counter to ripen at room temperature for 1 to 2 days, then place it in the fridge. Stored in the fridge, it may stay ripe for up to 1 month before it begins to sour.

Don't throw away the wilted cabbage leaves!

When I was a child and cooked with my grandmother on her farm, we always tried to use as much of everything as possible. Whenever we made this kimchi, we saved the discarded and wilted pieces of young cabbage to make soup. You can do the same: Place the leaves in a large pot, cover with water, and boil until the leaves are tender, about 10 minutes. Drain, then rinse the leaves in cold tap water—do not worry about residual liquid—and set aside.

Place a large pot on the stove and turn the heat to high. Add the cabbage leaves to the pot in 4-cup / 600g portions, and for every 4 cups / 600g cabbage, add 1½ teaspoons Gahreun Mahneul / Blended Garlic (page 49), 2 teaspoons Gahreun Saeoo Jut / Blended Salted Shrimp (page 128), 2 teaspoons fish sauce, 1½ teaspoons toasted sesame oil, and 2 or 3 pinches of ground black pepper. Mix with your hands until everything is well incorporated, then add ¼ cup / 30g thinly sliced yellow onions (about ¼ medium onion) and, if you'd like, one or two slices of jalapeño, and mix. Add 1 cup / 240ml water and boil for 5 minutes, then reduce the heat and simmer for another 20 minutes (the longer it cooks, the better it will taste). Garnish with 1 sliced green onion, ½ teaspoon toasted sesame seeds (page 51), and ½ teaspoon toasted sesame oil. It is delicious served with hot rice!

GLUTEN-FREE IF USING GLUTEN-FREE FISH SAUCE

박초이 김치

Bok Choy Kimchi

Makes 1 qt / 890g

Bok choy is not as common in Korea as it is in the United States, where it's readily available in most major supermarkets. I have found that it makes a tasty kimchi that, once prepared, can also be used to make a delicious banchan (see opposite). For that reason, I strongly suggest dividing this kimchi in half: Place half of it in an airtight container, store it in your fridge, and bring it out whenever you want some kimchi with your meal. Place the other half in a second airtight container and leave it to ferment at room temperature on your counter overnight. The next morning, its flavors will have deepened just enough to make the banchan.

- 1 lb / 450g bok choy (8 to 10 bunches)
- 2 teaspoons sea salt
- 3 tablespoons coarse gochugaru
- 2 tablespoons Gahreun Saeoo Jut / Blended Salted Shrimp (page 128)
- 2 tablespoons Gahreun Mahneul / Blended Garlic (page 49)
- 2 tablespoons fish sauce
- 1 tablespoon granulated sugar
- 1 teaspoon Gahreun Senggang / Blended Ginger (page 89)
- 1½ cups / 120g any combination of thinly sliced Korean chives, green onions (green and white parts), yellow onions, and red bell peppers, or red jalapeños (for spice)
- ½ cup / 30g thinly sliced minari (Korean watercress), about ½ bunch

1 Wash the bok choy, then slice the stems off each bunch. Place the leaves in a large bowl and sprinkle with the salt. Set aside for 20 to 30 minutes, then rinse the bok choy once in cold tap water and place in a colander for about 5 minutes to drain.

2 While the bok choy drains, use another large bowl to mix together the gochugaru, salted shrimp, garlic, fish sauce, sugar, and ginger. Add the bok choy and, using your hands, mix until well combined. Add the chives, green onions, yellow onions, bell peppers, and minari and mix again by hand. It's ready to serve right away. Alternatively, store the kimchi in an airtight 1-qt / 1L jar or other food-grade container and refrigerate. Depending on the temperature of your refrigerator, it could stay ripe for up to 1 week or so before it overripens and sours, at which point you can use it in Bok Choy Kimchi Chigae (opposite).

GLUTEN-FREE IF USING GLUTEN-FREE FISH SAUCE

Quick Bok Choy Kimchi Banchan

Makes about 2 cups / 445g

White vinegar and sesame oil are rarely used to make kimchi, since vinegar negatively affects the flavor, and sesame oil can create an environment for harmful bacteria during the long fermentation process. But for a quick banchan that you'll serve right away, these two ingredients perfectly complement the flavors of the ripe bok choy kimchi.

- 2 cups / 300g Bok Choy Kimchi (opposite)
- 2 tablespoons white vinegar, plus more to taste
- 2 tablespoons toasted sesame oil
- 1 tablespoon granulated sugar, plus more to taste
- 1 tablespoon toasted sesame seeds (page 51)

Combine the kimchi, vinegar, sesame oil, sugar, and sesame seeds in a large bowl. Taste and add additional vinegar and/or sugar to taste. Serve.

Bok Choy Kimchi Chigae

Serves 4

Bok choy kimchi is not usually part of most chigaes, but when your bok choy kimchi is overly fermented and is too sour to eat on its own, it's excellent as the main ingredient in the stew. Serve it with a bowl of hot steamed rice.

- 2 cups / 300g overripened Bok Choy Kimchi (opposite)
- 1½ cups / 360ml Anchovy and Dashi Broth (page 48) or store-bought, plus more as needed
- 1 tablespoon toasted sesame oil
  Chopped green onions, green and white parts, for garnish

Place a medium pot over high heat and add the kimchi, anchovy broth, and oil. Bring to a boil and cook for about 30 minutes, keeping the heat on high, or until the bok choy has softened and becomes translucent. As it cooks, the liquid will evaporate, so continually add 1 to 2 tablespoons and up to ½ cup / 120ml more anchovy broth as needed. Transfer to a serving bowl, garnish with the green onions, and serve with rice.

Cucumber Kimchi

Makes about 1 qt / 750g

This is a delicious, refreshing kimchi that is ready right away. The cucumbers are stuffed with a mixture of ginger, garlic, salted shrimp, carrots, onions, peppers, and chives. (Choose Korean chives when their leaves are especially thick and vibrant during the spring and summer; if they're not available in your area, Chinese chives can be used instead.) To make stuffing them easier, I slice the cucumbers into bite-sized pieces, rather than splitting the cucumber down the middle. The smaller pieces also have the advantage of being perfect to pass around during a party! If you prefer, you can simply slice the cucumbers into four large pieces and toss them with the filling. (Although this version isn't as pretty as the stuffed one, it is faster.) Korean and pickling cucumbers are ideal for this recipe; Persian cucumbers, on the other hand, will quickly lose their texture once stuffed. While the cucumbers are freshest when eaten right away, you can also stack them flat in an airtight glass container to ferment slightly.

- 1½ to 2 lb / 680 to 900g Korean or pickling cucumbers, sliced into 1½-inch / 4cm rounds
- 2¾ teaspoons granulated sugar
- 2 teaspoons sea salt
- 2 tablespoons coarse gochugaru
- 1 tablespoon Gahreun Mahneul / Blended Garlic (page 49)
- 1 tablespoon Gahreun Saeoo Jut / Blended Salted Shrimp (page 128)
- 1 tablespoon fish sauce
- ½ teaspoon Gahreun Senggang / Blended Ginger (page 89)
- ¼ cup / 15g thinly sliced Korean or Chinese chives (about ½ bunch)
- ¼ cup / 35g diced carrots (about ½ large carrot)
- ¼ cup / 30g diced yellow onions (about ¼ medium onion)
- ¼ cup / 40g diced red bell peppers (about ½ bell pepper)

1 Stand the cucumber pieces upright and cut a deep x through ¾ of the cucumber, being careful not to slice all the way down. Place the cucumbers in a colander set over a bowl and sprinkle ¾ teaspoon of the sugar and 1½ teaspoons of the salt over the pieces. Place a heavy weight, like a plate with canned food, on top and set aside for 30 to 45 minutes to allow the excess liquid to drain into the bowl.

2 Add the gochugaru, garlic, salted shrimp, fish sauce, remaining 1½ teaspoons sugar, ginger, and remaining ½ teaspoon salt to the drained liquid and stir until well mixed. Add the chives, carrots, onions, and bell peppers. Use your hands to mix until well incorporated. Stuff the mixture into the cross section of each cucumber piece.

3 After stuffing, serve immediately or place each piece in a 1-qt / 1L jar or other food-grade container with an airtight lid. Cover the container and leave at room temperature. When you start to see air bubbles in the liquid, refrigerate the kimchi. Serve the cucumbers right out of the refrigerator, when they're still cold and crisp. Enjoy the cucumbers soon after they're made; after a few days, they will begin to lose their texture and turn yellow and sour.

GLUTEN-FREE IF USING GLUTEN-FREE FISH SAUCE

YANGPA KIMCHI

양파 김치

Yellow Onion Kimchi

Makes 1 to 1½ qt / 600 to 900g

The crunch and spice of yellow onions make them the perfect kimchi to complement any Korean BBQ spread. If you find Korean chives with thick (about ¼ inch / 6mm) leaves, use them here; otherwise, Chinese chives will do just fine. Note there's a bit of spice here thanks to the jalapeños; for a milder banchan, remove the seeds from the chiles before slicing. I suggest letting the onions ferment at least overnight, but if you'd like to eat this kimchi right away, add a tablespoon or so of white vinegar before serving.

  2 lb / 900g medium yellow onions (2 to 3 onions), cut into 2½-inch / 6.5cm slices
  1 bunch Korean or Chinese chives, cut into 2½-inch / 6.5cm slices
  2 jalapeños, cut into 2½-inch / 6.5cm slices
  ¼ cup / 45g coarse gochugaru
  1½ teaspoons Gahreun Mahneul / Blended Garlic (page 49)
  1¼ teaspoons sea salt
  1¼ teaspoons fish sauce
  1¼ teaspoons Gahreun Saeoo Jut / Blended Salted Shrimp (page 128)
  1 teaspoon granulated sugar
  ¼ teaspoon Gahreun Senggang / Blended Ginger (page 89)

1 In a medium bowl, combine the onions, chives, and jalapeños.

2 In a large bowl, stir together ¼ cup plus 1 tablespoon / 75ml cold tap water with the gochugaru, garlic, salt, fish sauce, salted shrimp, sugar, and ginger. Add the onions, chives, and jalapeños to the bowl and mix well.

3 Transfer the mixture to a 1½- to 2-qt / 1.5 to 2L jar or other food-grade container with a lid and allow it to ferment until it's about as ripe as you'd like, then refrigerate. After transferring to the fridge, this kimchi will maintain its level of ripeness for 4 or 5 days before beginning to sour.

GLUTEN-FREE IF USING GLUTEN-FREE FISH SAUCE

SPINOFF

Once the kimchi is too ripe to eat on its own, use it as a great base for quick and spicy fried rice. To make, chop the kimchi into smaller pieces, toss the pieces into a hot pan oiled with a drizzle of toasted sesame oil, then sauté with day-old rice for a few minutes.

양배추 김치

Green Cabbage Kimchi

Makes about 2 qt / 1.1kg

This kimchi is very common at the many Korean-Chinese restaurants in Los Angeles. I love eating it with rice or noodles topped with jajang, the fermented black bean sauce, since its crunch and tang cuts right through the richness of the sauce. At home, I'll make this kimchi to serve alongside similarly bold dishes, like Braised Beef in Soy Sauce (page 118), Beef and Radish Soup (page 234), and Spicy Squid Soup (page 231). This kimchi is best when it is just slightly fermented and served cold. If you start it tonight, it will be ready by tomorrow.

- 2 lb / 900g green cabbage (1 small head)
- ¼ cup plus 3 tablespoons / 75g coarse gochugaru
- 3½ tablespoons granulated sugar
- 2 tablespoons Gahreun Mahneul / Blended Garlic (page 49)
- 1 tablespoon Gahreun Saeoo Jut / Blended Salted Shrimp (page 128)
- 1 tablespoon sea salt
- 1 tablespoon fish sauce
- ½ teaspoon Gahreun Senggang / Blended Ginger (page 89)
- ½ medium yellow onion, thinly sliced
- 1 bunch Chinese chives, cut into 1½-inch / 4cm slices
- 2 green onions, green and white parts, cut into 1½-inch / 4cm slices

1 Remove any wilted or tough outer leaves of the cabbage, then core and cut the cabbage into 1½-inch / 4cm slices.

2 In a large bowl, stir together 1 cup / 240ml cold tap water with the gochugaru, sugar, garlic, salted shrimp, salt, fish sauce, and ginger. Add the cabbage, yellow onions, chives, and green onions and mix well. Place the entire mixture in a 2-qt / 2L jar or other food-grade container with a lid and let it sit out on your countertop for 12 hours, or overnight, then refrigerate. Serve cold. It'll keep for up to 1 week.

GLUTEN-FREE IF USING GLUTEN-FREE FISH SAUCE

Other Family Favorites

This section is a collection of my favorite dishes—other than soon tofu, of course!—to make at home. Throughout, I make good use of the ingredients, marinades, and broths prepared in the earlier sections of the book. This is intentional: I try not to waste any food if I can help it, so when I cook or shop, I think about how I can make several meals out of the same ingredients and what I can do with any leftovers. For example, if you are wondering what else you can make with that batch of Anchovy and Dashi Broth (page 48) you made for soon tofu, or you have a jar of kimchi that is too ripe to eat on its own, you will find some ideas here. However you build your meal, be sure to include plenty of rice!

Appetizers

In Korean home cooking, all the dishes in a meal are typically served together at about the same time. I did the same at my restaurant, but in adapting my menu for Los Angeles I decided to add a selection of appetizers so my guests could have a snack while they waited for their order. I've included several of those appetizers here, as well as other appetizers like jeon (pancakes) that are part of my everyday home cooking, too. Most of these also can be easily doubled or tripled and passed around during a party, or served all by themselves as anju— snacks that go nicely with an iced cold drink.

NOKDOO BINDAEDDUK

녹두빈대떡

Mung Bean Pancakes

Serves 4 to 6

These crispy pancakes use savory mung beans as the base for the batter. This is a recipe I learned from my grandmother, who fried these up often when I visited her as a child. Nowadays I make these as comfort food for my mother. Use any ripe kimchi you have in your fridge—it's also a great way to use up any kimchi that is past its prime and too sour to eat on its own (overripe). The mung beans and sweet rice need to be soaked for a few hours, or overnight, before cooking (sweet rice is also called glutinous or sticky rice, and it's found in the same market aisle as other rice and grains). They will more than double in size as they absorb the water, so be sure to place both in a large enough bowl and use enough water. I add potato starch to the batter rather than corn or any other starch, as potato starch is what gives these pancakes a crackling crisp. To fry the pancakes, a pan you'd use for American-style pancakes will give you good-sized circles.

1½ **cups / 300g peeled mung beans**
2 **tablespoons sweet rice**
1 **large egg**
2 **tablespoons potato starch**
½ **teaspoon sea salt**
2 **cups / 300g chopped ripe kimchi**
1½ **teaspoons toasted sesame oil**
1½ **teaspoons Gahreun Mahneul /
Blended Garlic (page 49)**
1½ **teaspoons granulated sugar**
2 **cups / 160g mung bean sprouts, rinsed**
½ **cup / 60g sliced yellow onions
(a little less than ½ large onion)**
½ **cup / 115g sliced green onions, green
parts only, or Korean or Chinese chives**
1 **tablespoon chopped red bell pepper
Vegetable or other neutral oil, for frying
Soy Sauce Dip (page 165), for serving**

1 Place the mung beans and sweet rice in a large bowl and cover with 4 cups / 950ml water. Soak for at least 3 hours or overnight.

2 Drain and place the mung beans and sweet rice in a blender. Add 1 cup / 240ml water, the egg, potato starch, and salt and blend until nearly ssmooth. The mixture should be a little coarse and have some texture. Transfer to a large bowl and set aside.

3 In a medium bowl, combine the kimchi, sesame oil, garlic, and sugar, then add the mixture to the mung beans. Add the sprouts, yellow onions, green onions, and bell pepper. Using a spoon, gently mix everything together. Now it's ready to fry.

4 Place a pan over high heat and coat the pan with vegetable oil. When the oil starts to smoke, drop a few spoonfuls of the mixture into the pan (you can make your pancakes as small or as large or as thick or as thin as you'd like), and turn down the heat to medium. Fry until golden brown on one side, then flip and fry the other side. Repeat for the remainder of the batter, being sure to add as much vegetable oil as needed so each pancake is nice and crispy.

5 Place the pancakes on a platter or large plate and bring it out to your guests along with a big bowl of the soy sauce dip.

▶▶▶ **Make it meaty:** Pork, beef, or any other protein can be added to the pancake, too. Whichever protein you use, marinate it first: In a small bowl, combine 1 cup / 225g chopped meat with ½ teaspoon each of the following: sea salt, Gahreun Manheul / Blended Garlic (page 49), toasted sesame oil, and ground black pepper. If using pork, add ½ teaspoon Gahreun Senggang / Blended Ginger (page 89) as well. Place in the fridge and marinate for at least 30 minutes, then add to the batter after you add the kimchi.

▶▶▶ **Make it gluten-free:** Without the Soy Sauce Dip, these pancakes are gluten-free.

KIMCHI JEON

김치전

Kimchi Pancakes

Serves 4 to 6

If you have kimchi in your fridge now, kimchi pancakes are in your future. That's because when the kimchi ripens to a point where it is too sour to eat on its own, it is delicious repurposed as a filling for these pancakes; even the brine from the kimchi is incorporated into the batter. The pancakes are very easy to make, too. In fact, when I was in junior high school, I made kimchi pancakes all the time for my family and friends! Back then, I made them from scratch, but these days I take advantage of the prepared mixes found at most Asian markets to save time. Look for packages marked "Korean pancake mix" and "Korean frying mix." I have found that the combination of these two mixes, plus the addition of potato starch, produces the crispiest pancakes. You can, however, use only the pancake mix if that is what is available. With the time I save by not making the mix, I can season the kimchi with sesame oil and garlic before adding it to the batter. And while rice flour is optional, it also adds to the crispness. These pancakes are a delicious appetizer or snack to have with makgeolli, the milky sweet rice wine.

1 cup / 128g Korean pancake mix
1 cup / 128g Korean frying mix
½ cup / 80g potato starch
2 tablespoons rice flour (optional)
1 large egg
1 cup / 240ml unflavored sparkling water or still water
1½ cups / 225g chopped Spicy Napa Cabbage Kimchi (page 130) or store-bought, plus ⅓ cup / 80ml of the kimchi brine
1½ teaspoons toasted sesame oil
1½ teaspoons Gahreun Mahneul / Blended Garlic (page 49)
1½ teaspoons granulated sugar
1 teaspoon fish sauce
½ medium yellow onion, thinly sliced

1 tablespoon chopped jalapeño (optional)
1½ teaspoons coarse gochugaru (optional)
Vegetable or other neutral oil, for frying
Soy Sauce Dip, for serving (recipe follows)

1 In a large bowl, combine the pancake mix, frying mix, potato starch, rice flour (if using), egg, and sparkling water and stir until smooth.

2 In another large bowl, mix together the kimchi, sesame oil, garlic, sugar, and fish sauce, then add it to the batter along with the kimchi brine and onions and gently stir to combine. For more heat, add the jalapeño and/or the gochugaru (if using) and stir to incorporate.

3 Place a skillet over high heat and add 1 to 2 tablespoons vegetable oil. When the oil begins to smoke, spread a few spoonfuls of the batter into the pan. (How much will depend on how small or large you like your pancakes and the size of your pan; use more batter for larger pancakes and less for smaller ones.) Turn down the heat to medium and cook the pancake until golden brown on both sides. Repeat with the remaining batter, adding more vegetable oil between batches to ensure each pancake is nice and crispy.

4 These are great piping hot with the soy sauce dip.

▶▶▶ **Make it meaty:** You can also add ½ cup / 115g of any minced meat to the pancake batter. I recommend pork or beef since those proteins complement and bring out the flavor of the kimchi. Whichever meat you choose, marinate it first: In a small bowl, combine ½ teaspoon each of sea salt, Gahreun Mahneul / Blended Garlic (page 49), toasted sesame oil, and ground black pepper and, if you're using pork, ½ teaspoon Gahreun Senggang / Blended Ginger (page 89). Place in the fridge and marinate for at least 30 minutes, then add to the batter after you add the kimchi.

Soy Sauce Dip

Makes a little less than ¼ cup / 60ml

- 4½ teaspoons white vinegar
- 1 tablespoon soy sauce
- 1½ teaspoons granulated sugar
- 1½ teaspoons coarse gochugaru (optional)
- 1½ teaspoons chopped green onions, green and white parts (optional)
- 1½ teaspoons chopped jalapeño (optional)
- ½ teaspoon toasted sesame oil
- ½ teaspoon toasted sesame seeds (page 51)

Combine the vinegar, soy sauce, and sugar in a small bowl. Then, if using, add the gochugaru, green onions, and jalapeño. Add the oil and sesame seeds and mix. If you don't plan to use the sauce immediately, store it in an airtight container in the refrigerator. If you add the green onions or jalapeños, it will keep for up to 4 days. Without the vegetables, it will store well for up to 2 weeks. This recipe can easily be doubled or even tripled and stored for later use.

YANGNYUM DOOBOO

양념 두부

Soft Tofu in Soy Sauce with Seaweed

Serves 4 to 6

When I opened Beverly Soon Tofu, there were no Korean tofu manufacturers in the Los Angeles area. That changed in 1991, when Pulmuone entered the U.S. market with a subsidiary in Los Angeles. I was invited to their opening event, and there I saw one thing that really excited me: soon tofu in a tube. The only extra-soft tofu available at the time were cubes packed in boxes, but with Pulmuone's new product, the tofu could be sliced into circles! That simple change in aesthetic was enough to give me an idea for a light appetizer customers could enjoy while they waited for their soon tofu stew: tofu rounds seasoned with a sauce and topped with seaweed. I served it to my customers shortly after that event, and it was a hit!

Pulmuone is now well known in the United States. Their soon tofu is still packed in tubes and available at Korean markets. If it's not available where you live, you can, of course, use any brand of extra-soft tofu. Whichever brand you pick up, handle the tofu with care; extra-soft tofu is very delicate and falls apart easily.

1 (19-oz / 535g) package or 2 (11-oz / 310g) packages extra-soft tofu, preferably Pulmuone brand
Tofu Sauce (page 74)
Seasoned shredded seaweed or furikake, for garnish

1 Gently slice the delicate tofu into ½-inch / 12mm rounds and arrange them in one layer on a plate. Extra-soft tofu contains quite a bit of water, so I recommend draining it before adding the tofu sauce, or the water will dilute the sauce. To drain, set the rounds aside for a few minutes, then discard the water that collects on the plate. Wipe the plate dry or place the slices on a clean, dry plate.

2 Pour enough of the tofu sauce to cover most of the tofu. Garnish with a sprinkling of the seaweed and serve.

VEGETARIAN, VEGAN

▸▸▸ **To make a salad:** Lay shredded iceberg lettuce, cabbage, or green leaf lettuce on the plate and arrange the drained sliced tofu on top. Drizzle the tofu sauce over the plate and garnish with a sprinkling of the seaweed.

▸▸▸ **To make with kimchi:** Slice ½ cup / 75g ripe kimchi into ½-inch / 12mm pieces and place in a bowl with ½ teaspoon toasted sesame oil, ½ teaspoon toasted sesame seeds (page 51), and ½ teaspoon granulated sugar. Mix to combine, then layer the kimchi on top of the drained sliced tofu. Finish with half of the tofu sauce and garnish with a sprinkling of the seaweed.

김치 두부 스테이크

Tofu Steak with Kimchi

Serves 4

I added different appetizers to my restaurant's menu over the years; this one made its debut on the Beverly Soon Tofu menu in the early 2000s. It is my twist on a popular dish in Korea called tofu kimchi, which is often served as an anju, a snack served with alcohol. Tofu kimchi contains tofu, kimchi, and usually pork. For my version, I omit the pork, dredge the tofu in potato starch to give it an especially crispy exterior when pan-fried, then add a soy sauce dressing and a sprinkle of seaweed shreds. The kimchi is then served sizzling in a hot cast-iron skillet.

- 1 (19-oz / 538g) package firm tofu, preferably House Foods brand, sliced into halves lengthwise
- ¼ cup / 45g potato starch
- 4 tablespoons / 60ml vegetable or other neutral oil, plus more for frying
- 2 cups / 300g ripe or overripe kimchi
- 2 or 3 drops plus 1 teaspoon toasted sesame oil
- 2 tablespoons Tofu Sauce (page 74)
- 2 tablespoons seasoned shredded seaweed or furikake, plus more to taste
- 1 teaspoon toasted sesame seeds (page 51), for garnish

1 Place the tofu in a colander set over a bowl and drain for 10 to 15 minutes, then pat the pieces as dry as possible with a paper towel.

2 Place the potato starch in a medium bowl. Add the tofu and dredge on all sides. Line a large plate with paper towels and set next to the stove.

3 Place a medium frying pan over medium heat and add 2 tablespoons of the vegetable oil. When the oil begins to smoke, place the tofu in the pan in one layer, being careful since any remaining moisture in the tofu will cause the oil to spatter. Pan-fry until golden brown, then flip. Continue to pan-fry until all sides of the tofu are golden brown, adding more vegetable oil as necessary as you flip and rotate each piece, 8 to 10 minutes total. Remove the cooked tofu from the pan and place on the paper towel–lined plate to collect the excess oil.

4 In a sauté pan, add the remaining 2 tablespoons vegetable oil along with the kimchi. Sauté until the kimchi is cooked through and its color is translucent, 5 to 8 minutes. Add the 2 or 3 drops of sesame oil and remove from the heat.

5 Set a trivet on the table. Place a small cast-iron skillet or griddle over high heat and remove the pan from the heat once it is hot. Place the kimchi in the pan in one layer, then place the tofu on top of the kimchi. Add the tofu sauce and seaweed on top. Drizzle the remaining 1 teaspoon sesame oil over the tofu, garnish with the sesame seeds, and carefully bring it to the table and set it down on the trivet to serve.

VEGETARIAN, VEGAN IF USING VEGAN KIMCHI

TOFU BUCHIM

두부 부침

Pan-Fried Tofu with Dipping Sauce

Serves 4

You probably won't be surprised to know that I always have tofu in my refrigerator. Whenever I have unexpected guests, I pull out a package or two to make this simple, unfussy dish. I love it for several reasons: It takes no time at all to lightly pan-fry the tofu and stir together a dipping sauce, it appeals to both vegetarians and non-vegetarians alike, and it gives my guests something to snack on as we chat, while I get a few other dishes on the stove. Be sure to use extra-firm tofu here so the pieces keep their structure as they fry. My preferred brand is House Foods, whose label for its extra-firm tofu is bright red for easy identification. Serve the tofu with ice-cold drinks like soju or makgeolli.

- 1 (19-oz / 538g) package extra-firm tofu, preferably House Foods brand
- 2 tablespoons vegetable or other neutral oil
  Dipping Sauce (recipe follows), for serving

1 Dice the tofu into 16 equally sized pieces. (If your package contains 4 large blocks of tofu, you just need to quarter each of those blocks to create 16 cubes.)

2 Place the tofu in a colander set over a bowl to release some of the liquid for 10 to 15 minutes, then pat the pieces as dry as possible with a paper towel.

3 Line a large plate with a few layers of paper towels and place next to your stove. Place a large nonstick frying pan over high heat and add the oil. When the oil begins to smoke, place the tofu in the pan very carefully, since any remaining moisture in the tofu will cause the oil to spatter.

4 Pan-fry until golden brown, then flip. Continue to pan-fry until all sides of the tofu are golden brown, 2 to 3 minutes total. Transfer to the paper towel–lined plate to collect the excess oil, then place on a platter. Serve with the dipping sauce—and the drinks!

VEGETARIAN, VEGAN

Dipping Sauce

Makes about ½ cup / 120ml

- 1 bunch green onions, green and white parts, chopped
- ¼ cup / 60ml soy sauce
- 3 tablespoons rice cooking wine
- 1 tablespoon Gahreun Mahneul / Blended Garlic (page 49)
- 1 tablespoon chopped jalapeño
- 1 tablespoon toasted sesame oil
- 2 teaspoons toasted sesame seeds (page 51)
- 1 teaspoon coarse gochugaru

Place all the ingredients in a small bowl and mix together. Serve immediately or store in an airtight container in the refrigerator for up to 3 days.

VEGETARIAN, VEGAN

DONGEULANGDENG

동그랑땡

Beef and Pork Patties

Serves 4 to 6

Koreans may not be especially known for meat patties, but they are a big part of our home cooking. In fact, my sister has been making this dish for over thirty-five years! It's one of her favorite dishes to make because it's inexpensive, festive enough to be served at parties, and can be made ahead of time. Kids like these meat patties, too—they were one of my nephew's favorite dishes—and kids won't even know you've snuck plenty of vegetables into the mix. My sister serves the patties with a salad of shredded cabbage tossed with homemade Thousand Island dressing. I also highly recommend topping the patties with a few squeezes from the orange-labeled Bull-Dog Vegetable and Fruit Sauce that is available at most Asian markets.

½   lb / 225g ground beef
½   lb / 225g ground pork
3   tablespoons toasted sesame oil
3   tablespoons granulated sugar
4½ teaspoons Gahreun Mahneul / Blended Garlic (page 49)
1½ teaspoons ground black pepper
1   teaspoon sea salt
1   teaspoon fish sauce
1   teaspoon soy sauce
½   teaspoon Gahreun Senggang / Blended Ginger (page 89)
4   oz / 28g button or cremini mushrooms, chopped
3   cups / 420g minced yellow onions (2 large or 3 medium onions)
1   cup / 160g minced green onions, green and white parts
½   cup / 60g chopped zucchini (about ½ medium zucchini)
½   cup / 79g chopped carrots (about ½ medium carrot)
4   medium eggs
1   cup / 60g panko breadcrumbs
2   tablespoons Korean pancake mix
2   tablespoons potato starch
    Vegetable oil, for frying
    Bull-Dog Vegetable and Fruit Sauce, for serving
    Shredded green cabbage, for serving
    Thousand Island dressing (or your preferred dressing), for serving

1 In a large bowl, add the beef, pork, sesame oil, sugar, garlic, black pepper, salt, fish sauce, soy sauce, and ginger and mix together with a wooden spoon or other large spoon. Set aside for 10 to 15 minutes to marinate.

2 Add the mushrooms, yellow onions, green onions, zucchini, and carrots to the meat mixture and, using your spoon, stir to incorporate. Add the eggs, panko, pancake mix, and potato starch and, using your hands (and gloves, if you like), incorporate all the ingredients well.

3 Pinch off a small piece of the meat mixture, roll it into a ball, throw it back into the bowl, then pick it up and throw it back again, then again, one more time. This technique will tenderize the meat, knock out any air pockets, and keep the meatball tacky so it adheres to itself and keeps its shape. Set the meatball aside in the bowl or on a separate plate and continue forming meatballs with the rest of the mixture.

4 Place a large frying pan over medium heat and add about 2 tablespoons vegetable oil. Using the palm of your hand or the bottom of a clean glass, flatten a few meatballs into thick, round patties. When the oil begins to smoke, carefully slide the patties into the oil, being careful not to crowd the pan. Keeping the heat at medium—if the heat is too high, the patties will burn on one side and not cook through—fry until golden brown, then flip. Fry the other side until it's also golden brown and the meat is cooked through. (I usually make mine about ¼ inch / 6mm thick and fry for 3 to 5 minutes per side.)

5 Repeat with the remaining meat mixture, wiping the pan with a paper towel and liberally adding enough vegetable oil between batches. Top the patties with a few squeezes of sauce. Mix the the cabbage with salad dressing and offer the salad alongside the patties.

Large Platters to Share

The dishes in this section—marinated meats seared on the grill and delivered to the table; sizzling, colorful bowls of bibimbap; a hot pot full of meat, fresh vegetables, and tofu—are extremely versatile. Pick one or two and include them as part of a big spread of rice, banchan, kimchi, and a soup or stew. Or, choose one and make it a meal with a bowl of rice, banchan, and kimchi. As these dishes lend themselves to sharing, many can be prepared ahead of time and brought to a gathering. I also offer a few ideas for building a party around a tabletop grill or a buffet of ingredients where guests can make their own bibimbaps. Several dishes in this section are home versions of the most popular shared platters I offered at Beverly Soon Tofu. These were perennial crowd favorites that I'm sure will be a big hit in your home, too.

미나리 사라다

Minari Salad with Soy Sauce Vinaigrette

Serves 6 to 8

During the late spring and early summer when minari (Korean watercress) is at its best, I always make this salad to serve alongside platters of Korean BBQ. The minari's bright, peppery flavor makes it a great side to complement the heavy meats, but the salad also stands on its own if you want a meal of mostly greens, with just a bit of the BBQ on the side. Minari can be found in many Korean and Asian markets, especially when it's in season. When shopping, look for long, crisp stems and vibrant bright green leaves. Avoid bunches that look limp or those with leaves that have begun to yellow or brown. If the stems are tough and stringy or if it's not available, you can use thinly sliced leeks, Asian chives, red onion, kale, or napa cabbage instead. For the rest of the salad, I use cucumbers and kkaetnip (perilla leaves), a summertime green; shredded green onions (see page 27); and crisp leaves of lettuce (when shopping, look for leaves that appear moist rather than dry, since they are the freshest). The exact amount of each ingredient varies, as I'll use more green onions, for example, when they're especially green at the market, and maybe fewer cucumbers if they're not as fresh. I've left room in my recipe to allow you to be flexible as well.

As you assemble the salad, be sure each green is completely dry; otherwise, the vinaigrette will not adhere and the vegetables will be unevenly coated. Because this salad is best when everything is crisp and fresh, set your table first. Then, when you're just about ready to eat, dress the salad and serve. Leftover vinaigrette is delicious over any other bowl of greens.

- **1 to 2 Persian or Korean cucumbers, thinly sliced**
- **1 to 2 bunches kkaetnip (perilla leaves), shredded**
- **1 bunch minari (Korean watercress), chopped into 2-inch / 5cm pieces**
- **1 to 2 bunches green onions, shredded or finely sliced**
- **2 to 3 heads green leaf lettuce, red leaf lettuce, or a combination of both, shredded**
  Soy Sauce Vinaigrette (recipe follows)
  Toasted sesame seeds (page 51), for garnish

1 Place the cucumbers in a colander set over a bowl to drain for 15 minutes.

2 Dab the cucumbers dry with a paper towel and place them in a large bowl along with the kkaetnip, minari, green onions, and lettuces.

3 Add enough vinaigrette to coat the vegetables, then toss. Garnish with the sesame seeds and serve immediately.

VEGETARIAN, VEGAN

CONTINUED

Soy Sauce Vinaigrette

Makes about 1½ cups / 360ml

- 1 cup / 240ml Mat Ganjang / Seasoned Soy Sauce (page 88)
- ¼ cup plus 1 tablespoon / 75ml white vinegar, plus more to taste
- 2 tablespoons rice cooking wine
- 2 tablespoons Gahreun Mahneul / Blended Garlic (page 49)
- 2 tablespoons toasted sesame seeds (page 51)
- 1 tablespoon toasted sesame oil
- 1 tablespoon coarse gochugaru
- ½ teaspoon ground black pepper

Combine the seasoned soy sauce, vinegar, cooking wine, garlic, sesame seeds, sesame oil, gochugaru, and black pepper in a medium bowl and mix well. Taste and add additional vinegar or a few spoonfuls of water if desired. The vinaigrette is ready to use immediately or can be poured into an airtight container and refrigerated for up to 1 week.

KIMCHI BOKKEUMBAP
김치 볶음밥
Kimchi Fried Rice

Serves 4

Kimchi fried rice is a great way to make good use of leftover white rice and older, overripe kimchi. I do specify short-grain white rice for this dish because I think white rice best absorbs the kimchi's flavors, but you can use whatever you have on hand. For a successful fry, the rice should be at least a day old, after it has lost some of its moisture. The other trick to making this fried rice as delicious as possible is to layer in other flavors as it cooks. I combine garlic with chopped bacon as it crisps, for example, and sauté green onions in the bacon fat, resulting in an infused oil that I then use to fry the rice and other ingredients. Finally, the bowl is topped with a runny egg. Kimchi fried rice is very popular and can be made in so many ways. I hope you enjoy this one.

- 2 **tablespoons vegetable or other neutral oil**
- 4 **large eggs**
- 4 **slices applewood smoked bacon**
- 1½ **cups / 225g kimchi, preferably overripened**
- 1 **teaspoon Gahreun Mahneul / Blended Garlic (page 49)**
- 1 **bunch chopped green onions, green and white parts**
- 4 **cups / 900g cooked short-grain white rice, at least 1 day old**
- 1 **tablespoon toasted sesame oil**
- ½ **teaspoon fish sauce**
- 1 **tablespoon toasted sesame seeds (page 51), for garnish**

1 Place a large skillet or sauté pan over medium heat and add the vegetable oil. When the oil begins to smoke, crack the eggs into the pan and fry until the whites are set and the yolks are as you like them (I like my eggs sunny side up). Set aside.

2 Line a plate with paper towels and place next to your stove. Chop the bacon and kimchi into small, thin pieces for easy frying. Return the pan to the stove and set over high heat. Add the bacon and fry for a minute or two, just enough to render the fat. Add the garlic and fry until the bacon is crispy, a few more minutes. Remove the bacon mixture and set aside on the plate to drain.

3 Add 1 cup / 160g of the green onions to the pan and sauté. Add the kimchi and continue to sauté and stir until the white part of the kimchi turns translucent, 3 to 5 minutes. Add the rice and stir to incorporate, then mix in the sesame oil and fish sauce.

4 Return the bacon mixture to the pan and continue to sauté until everything is well combined. Garnish with the remaining 1 tablespoon green onions and the sesame seeds and divide the fried rice into bowls. Top each with a fried egg and serve hot.

GLUTEN-FREE IF USING GLUTEN-FREE FISH SAUCE

Bibimbap

The word *bibimbap* literally translates to "mixed rice," and that's exactly what it is: a rice bowl mixed with all sorts of ingredients, including lots of vegetables and your choice of protein. It's filling all on its own or delicious when served with soon tofu and other dishes. Depending on how many ingredients you include, bibimbap can take a little bit or a lot of time to make. But the process is rewarding, and it's a great dish to share with friends (see page 190).

My bibimbap is influenced by the version I used to eat with my grandmother at her temple. My grandmother was a Buddhist, and when I was a child, I spent the summers with her at her home in the countryside. My mother and I often joined her on her twice-monthly visits to her temple, which was located up in a mountainous area. Even at that young age, I was struck by the simplicity of the food. The land around the temple was verdant, and the monks created simple, nourishing soups and other dishes out of root vegetables and foraged herbs. They also had jars of dried vegetables to supplement their daily meals, and they made their own tofu.

Of all the dishes I ate there over many summers, the one that really stayed with me was the temple's bibimbap. The monks filled their rice bowls with what they grew and foraged, seasoning the fresh vegetables very lightly to let their full flavors shine through. To complete the bowl, they added kimchi and dried vegetables that had been rehydrated in water. And they added one ingredient that I have not seen in many other bibimbap: twigak, or sea kelp, that they dried and then fried. The fried kelp brought a delicious crunch and slight brininess to the rice bowl, and I still remember it to this day.

My grandmother incorporated fried twigak into her bibimbap, too. She also added meat, sometimes left over from a previous meal, in addition to the vegetables she picked from her garden and anything she may have dried or preserved.

My own bibimbap is based on those childhood experiences, although unlike my grandmother and the monks, I am very fortunate to have access to a variety of vibrant fresh produce in Los Angeles year round. With the exception of twigak and kimchi, then, all the vegetables I use are fresh. But like the monks, I keep the vegetables mildly seasoned, so I can better appreciate the flavors of the season.

Bibimbap is very personal, and it can easily be adjusted to suit your own taste and diet. Use my recipes as starting points and be creative with your own bibimbap. One of the hallmarks of bibimbap are the fresh vegetables, so use what is available to you. Add different types of kimchi for different bursts of acidity. And you can even toss in any meat or banchan you may have left over in your fridge.

My preferred way to make bibimbap is in a dolsot (see page 27). Made of stone, like agalmatolite or, more commonly, granite, dolsots have many uses in your kitchen. Like ttukbaegi, dolsots can go from the stove to the table, and they retain heat exceptionally well. When you assemble bibimbap in a hot dolsot, the rice will become nice and crisp, and the vegetables will sizzle and brown slightly.

My bibimbap recipes serve four. Dolsots large enough to serve four are difficult to find, so I use two dolsots with a diameter of about 9½ inches / 24cm that offer a good amount of surface area for the rice to crisp. Korean kitchen supply stores carry dolsots in that unique size. If you can't find one, dolsots are more widely available in small, medium, and large sizes; while the exact measurements may vary depending on the manufacturer, a large dolsot is usually big enough for two. You will find those at Korean markets, many Asian markets, and online (see page 239), and they usually include a trivet. I don't recommend dolsots any smaller than those, because you lose too much of the surface area, resulting in less-crispy rice. Note that dolsots should be seasoned before using. The method is the same as the seasoning method for ttukbaegi (see page 33). After a dolsot is seasoned, remember to oil it each time you use it before adding any ingredients.

You also can make the bibimbap in a large cast-iron skillet. A 10-inch / 25cm skillet will serve two; a 12-inch / 30cm or larger one will be big enough to serve four.

DOLPAN BIBIMBAP

돌판 비빔밥

Stone Pot Bibimbap with Mixed Vegetables

Serves 4

This bibimbap combines crunch from lettuce, fried sea kelp, and seasoned seaweed; spice from the gochujang; and sweet and savory notes from all the colorful vegetables. To round it out, tofu and beef are added, though you can easily make it completely vegetarian by omitting the meat, or vegan by omitting the meat and eggs. Like many bibimbap, this one does require a bit of prep work; to save you some time, I suggest using a mandoline to cut the vegetables into uniform pieces that will cook evenly. You also can cook the tofu and vegetables ahead of time. If you do so, store them in separate airtight containers in the fridge until it's time to assemble the dish. When you're ready to make the bibimbap, I suggest using two large dolsots about 9½ inches / 24cm in diameter. Alternatively, use two 10-inch / 25cm cast-iron skillets or combine everything into one 12-inch / 30cm or larger cast-iron skillet.

Beef

- 6 to 8 oz / 170 to 225g rib eye, short rib trimmings, or any other cut of beef with a bit of fat
- 1 teaspoon soy sauce
- 1 teaspoon Gahreun Mahneul / Blended Garlic (page 49)
- 1 teaspoon toasted sesame oil
- 1 teaspoon granulated sugar
- 1 teaspoon rice cooking wine
- ¼ teaspoon ground black pepper

Tofu and Vegetables

- 9½ oz / 269g medium or firm tofu (preferably House Foods brand)
- 1 cup / 80g soybean sprouts, rinsed
- ½ teaspoon sea salt, plus more for boiling water and sautéing
- 1 tablespoon plus 2½ teaspoons vegetable or other neutral oil, plus more for boiling water and greasing the pan
- ¼ small head red cabbage
- 1 medium carrot
- 1 small or ½ medium mu (Korean radish)
- ½ large zucchini
- 3 or 4 Persian cucumbers
- 1 teaspoon Gahreun Mahneul / Blended Garlic (page 49)
- 2 medium or large eggs

- 2   tablespoons toasted sesame oil, plus more for garnish
- 4   cups / 900g cooked short-grain white rice
- 1   cup / 30g Twigak / Fried Sea Kelp (page 108)
- 2   heads of green leaf lettuce, cut into ¼-inch / 6mm slices
- ½   cup / 10g seasoned shredded or crushed seaweed or furikake, for garnish Bibimbap Gochujang Sauce (recipe follows), for serving

1 TO PREPARE THE BEEF: Slice the beef into ½-inch / 12mm pieces and place in a large bowl. Add the soy sauce, garlic, sesame oil, sugar, cooking wine, and black pepper. Marinate the beef for 15 to 20 minutes while you prepare the tofu and vegetables.

2 TO PREPARE THE TOFU AND VEGETABLES: Pat the tofu dry with paper towels and set aside.

3 Place a large pot over high heat and add 1 cup / 240ml water. After the water comes to a boil, drop in the sprouts and boil for 3 minutes, then carefully taste the yellow tip of a sprout: raw sprouts often have a fishy flavor or aroma that should disappear once boiled properly. If the sprout still has a bit of fishiness to it, continue to boil on high for another 2 to 4 minutes, until it tastes only of the sprout. Be careful not to overboil the sprouts; they should be tender but still retain a crunch. Rinse the sprouts in cold tap water and place in a colander to dry.

4 Fill the same pot with 4 to 5 cups / 950ml to 1.2L water and place over high heat. Add a pinch of salt and a few drops of vegetable oil. Core the cabbage and shred into ¼-inch / 6mm slices. Once the water comes to a boil, add the cabbage and boil for 30 seconds, then immediately rinse with cold tap water. Place the cabbage in another colander to drain.

5 Slice the carrot, radish, zucchini, and cucumbers into ¼-inch / 6mm matchsticks and set aside. Keep the vegetables separated; don't mix them just yet.

6 Place a large skillet over high heat and add ½ teaspoon of the vegetable oil. When the oil begins to shimmer, carefully add the carrots along with a pinch of salt. Sauté the carrots just until they are soft, 20 to 30 seconds, then remove to a plate or bowl and set aside.

7 Wipe the pan clean and return it to the stove. Add 1 teaspoon of the vegetable oil. When the oil begins to shimmer, carefully add the radish, ½ teaspoon of the garlic, and ¼ teaspoon of the salt. Sauté until the radish is soft, 20 to 30 seconds, then remove to a plate or bowl.

8 Wipe the pan clean again and place it over the burner. Add 1 teaspoon of the vegetable oil, the zucchini, the remaining ½ teaspoon garlic, and the remaining ¼ teaspoon salt. Sauté until the zucchini is soft, 20 to 30 seconds, then transfer to a plate or bowl.

9 Wipe the pan clean again and place it over the burner. Add 1 tablespoon of the vegetable oil. When the oil begins to smoke, carefully add the tofu and brown on both sides. Set aside to cool, then cut into ½-inch / 12mm slices.

10 NOW, COOK THE BEEF AND EGGS. Wipe the pan clean and place it over high heat. When a drop of water sizzles in the pan, add the beef and sauté until the pieces are at your desired level of doneness. Remove.

CONTINUED

11 Wipe the pan clean one more time and add a few drops of vegetable oil. When the oil is hot, crack in the eggs and cook, sunny side up, until the yolks are cooked the way you like. Set aside.

12 FINALLY, CRISP THE RICE AND ASSEMBLE THE BIBIMBAP. Place the dolsots (or cast-iron skillets) over high heat and heat until they're very hot, 5 to 7 minutes. Add 1 tablespoon of the sesame oil to each and swirl it around to coat the entire interior. Divide the cooked rice in half and pack into two rice bowls. Flip each bowl onto the center of each dolsot so that the rice is in the shape of a domed mound. Arrange half of the sprouts, cabbage, carrots, radish, zucchini, cucumbers, tofu, and beef, and a handful of sea kelp in a circle around the rice in one dolsot and the rest of the vegetables, tofu, and beef, and another handful of sea kelp in the other dolsot (if there's any remaining sea kelp, place it in a bowl and share it at the table as banchan). Cook until the bottom of the rice is lightly browned and nice and crispy, 10 to 15 minutes. Each dolsot will serve two guests. (If you're using a cast-iron skillet large enough to fit all the rice, there's no need to divide the ingredients: you can assemble the entire bibimbap in that one skillet.) Have trivets or other heatproof settings at the table.

13 Carefully transfer the hot dolsots to their trivets, turning the pots so their handles are perpendicular to the handles on the trivets. (This may sound counterintuitive, but the dolsots' handles in this position will cool faster than if their handles were parallel with the trivets'.)

14 Place half of the lettuce in the center of one dolsot, on top of the rice, and the remaining half in the center of the other. Top with a fried egg. (For one cast-iron skillet, place all the sliced lettuce into the center and top with both fried eggs.) Add the shredded seaweed and finish with a bit of sesame oil over everything.

15 Bring the bibimbap and bibimbap sauce to the table and encourage your guests to add as much sauce as they'd like before mixing everything together. And remember: more sauce means more heat!).

▶▶▶ **To make this vegetarian,** omit the beef. Add extra tofu as desired.

▶▶▶ **To make this vegan,** omit the beef and egg. Add extra tofu as desired.

▶▶▶ **You also can assemble the bibimbap in rice bowls rather than dolsots.** The rice won't be crisped, but the bibimbap as a whole will feel a little lighter and more refreshing. To do so, divide the ingredients neatly among four rice bowls, and slide a fried egg on top of each. Because the toppings are so colorful and lively, I like to bring the bowls to the table so guests can eat with their eyes first, before they mix everything themselves. Serve with the bibimbap gochujang sauce.

Bibimbap Gochujang Sauce

Makes 1½ cups / 476ml

  1 cup / 380g gochujang
  ½ cup / 100g granulated sugar
  ¼ cup / 60ml rice cooking wine

Combine the gochujang, sugar, cooking wine, and ¼ cup / 60ml water in a medium bowl and stir well. Leftovers can be stored in an airtight container and refrigerated for up to 1 week.

TOFU KIMCHI DOLPAN BIBIMBAP

두부 김치 돌판 비빔밥

Stone Pot Bibimbap with Tofu and Kimchi

Serves 4

Tofu and extra-ripe kimchi are perfect companions in this bibimbap, and the rice, crisped in dolsots or cast-iron skillets, adds extra texture and flavor. Be sure to sear and cool the tofu before you slice it. If the tofu is too warm, it will fall apart. To make the bibimbap, use two large dolsots about 9½ inches / 24cm in diameter, two 10-inch / 25cm cast-iron skillets, or combine everything into one 12-inch / 30cm or larger cast-iron skillet.

- 2 cups / 300g ripe or overripe kimchi, cut into ½-inch / 12mm pieces
- 2 tablespoons plus 1 teaspoon toasted sesame oil, plus more for finishing
- 1 teaspoon granulated sugar
- 1 tablespoon vegetable or other neutral oil, plus more for frying
- 1 (19-oz / 538g) package medium or firm tofu, preferably House Foods brand, drained
- 4 cups / 900g cooked rice
- 2 medium or large eggs
- 2 heads green leaf lettuce, cut into ¼-inch / 6mm slices
- ½ cup / 10g seasoned shredded seaweed or furikake, for garnish
  Bibimbap Gochujang Sauce (page 185), for serving

1 Place a large skillet over medium heat and add the kimchi, 1 teaspoon of the sesame oil, the sugar, and ¼ cup / 60ml water. Sauté until the kimchi is translucent and cooked through, 6 to 8 minutes. Remove the kimchi and place it in a bowl.

2 Wipe the pan clean and return it to the stove. Over high heat, add the vegetable oil to the pan. When the oil is hot, add the tofu and brown it on all sides. Set the tofu aside and when it has cooled, cut it into ½-inch / 12mm pieces (if your tofu package contains 4 large cubes of tofu, you can simply slice each piece in half horizontally).

3 Place the dolsots (or cast-iron skillets) over high heat and heat until they're very hot, 5 to 7 minutes. Add 1 tablespoon of the sesame oil to each and swirl it around to coat the entire interior. Divide the cooked rice in half and pack it into two rice bowls. Flip each bowl onto the center of each dolsot so that the rice is in the shape of a domed mound.

4 Working with one dolsot at a time, quickly arrange the tofu slices in a circle around the rice, then place the kimchi around the tofu. Repeat until all the tofu and kimchi have been placed, or until the surfaces of the pots are completely covered. Each dolsot will serve two guests. (If you're using a cast-iron skillet large enough to fit all the rice, there's no need to divide the ingredients: you can assemble the entire bibimbap in that one skillet.) Have trivets or other heatproof settings ready at the table.

5 Leave the dolsots over high heat until the rice is crispy, 10 to 15 minutes. Carefully transfer the hot dolsots to their trivets, turning the pots so their handles are perpendicular to the handles on the trivets. (This may sound counterintuitive, but the dolsots' handles in this position will cool faster than if their handles were parallel with the trivets'.)

6 Wipe the pan from earlier clean and add a few drops of vegetable oil. When the oil is hot, crack in the eggs and cook, sunny side up, until the yolks are cooked the way you like. Set aside.

7 Place half the lettuce in the center of one dolsot, on top of the rice, and the remaining half in the center of the other. Top with a fried egg. (If you are using one cast-iron skillet, place all the lettuce in the center of the skillet and top with both fried eggs.) Garnish with the seaweed and finish with the sesame oil.

8 Bring the bibimbap and bibimbap sauce to the table and encourage your guests to add as much sauce as they'd like before mixing everything together. And remember: more sauce means more heat!

VEGETARIAN IF USING VEGETARIAN KIMCHI

▶▶▶ **You also can assemble the bibimbap in rice bowls rather than dolsots.** The rice won't be crisped, but the bibimbap as a whole will feel a little lighter and more refreshing. To do so, divide the ingredients neatly among four rice bowls, and slide a fried egg on top of each. Because the toppings are so colorful and lively, I like to bring the bowls to the table so guests can eat with their eyes first, before they mix everything themselves. Serve the bowls with the bibimbap gochujang sauce.

BIBIMBAP PARTY

Because it is so endlessly customizable, bibimbap is great for a party. Prepare each ingredient separately and place in individual serving bowls so everyone can pick and choose their own fillings. You can work together with your family and friends to prepare the ingredients or have everything cooked and ready for the group before they arrive. In either case, everyone will have a lot of fun building their own bibimbap bowl.

A few tips and ideas for your bibimbap party:

- I use steamed white rice in my bibimbap. If you have guests who prefer other grain options, you can offer brown or multigrain rice, too.

- As you shop for the party, remember the best-tasting vegetables are generally the ones in season.

- For bibimbap, most vegetables don't need a complex preparation. Most will be delicious sautéed in a little oil and seasoned with a bit of garlic and salt. Mushrooms especially are fantastic prepared this way.

- Part of the fun of bibimbap is its presentation. Choose a variety of colorful vegetables to include in your bowls.

- Slice or chop jalapeños for the table. That is a great option for those who would like more heat without adding more gochujang sauce.

Round out the bibimbap party with plenty of banchan and kimchi. If you want to make an entire spread, add a soup or a stew, plus a meat dish or two.

잡채

Japchae

Serves 4

Los Angeles is home to many different cultures, and I've adapted many of my recipes based on the flavors and ingredients I have found around me. This recipe came about during the pandemic. It was the last new dish we added to our menu at Beverly Soon Tofu before we closed.

Japchae is a dish I often make for family gatherings. In the past, I prepared japchae the classic way, using dangmyeon, glass noodles made with sweet potato starch. But not too long after Beverly Soon Tofu switched to takeout-only, I was at a restaurant supply store and happened to come across the thin, flat rice noodles used in many Vietnamese and Thai dishes. At that point, we did not yet have japchae on the menu, but it occurred to me that using rice rather than glass noodles would be a good way to make japchae takeout-friendly. Although rice noodles aren't as chewy and elastic as glass noodles, they carry sauce well. Crucially, unlike glass noodles, rice noodles can sit for a period of time without clumping and can be easily reheated in a microwave or pan. After testing the recipe with my family, we added it to our menu in May of 2020.

We closed in September of that year, but during those last four months, the japchae was popular with our customers, who enjoyed it at home with their soon tofu. I still make this version for myself and my family. Rice noodles are now quite common at major supermarkets, and Asian grocers offer a large variety. For this recipe, look for thin, flat noodles that may be labeled as rice vermicelli, rice sticks, or pad Thai noodles. If you prefer, you can replace the rice noodles with an equal amount of dangmyeon. Those noodles are available at Korean markets. The vegetables, too, are very customizable. I use cabbage, broccoli, cauliflower, and bell peppers, but feel free to use whatever you have in your refrigerator. Because this is a stir-fry, be sure to prepare your vegetables ahead of time and have them all ready to cook.

CONTINUED

2 tablespoons vegetable or other neutral oil

1 cup / 120g sliced yellow onions (about 1 medium onion)

1 cup / 140g thinly sliced carrot (1 to 2 large carrots)
Sea salt

1 cup / 50g shredded green cabbage (about ¼ medium cabbage)

1 cup / 50g shredded red cabbage (about ¼ medium cabbage)

½ cup / 50g broccoli florets (about ¼ medium broccoli)

½ cup / 50g cauliflower florets (about ¼ medium cauliflower)

1 (16-oz / 450g) package dried flat thin rice noodles, soaked for 2 hours or according to the manufacturer's instructions and then drained

½ cup / 120ml Mat Ganjang / Seasoned Soy Sauce (page 88)

4½ teaspoons Gahreun Mahneul / Blended Garlic (page 49)

1 tablespoon granulated sugar

1 cup / 60g sliced mushrooms (use whichever kind you like)

½ cup / 30g sliced (about 2 inches / 5cm) Korean or Chinese chives (about 1 bunch)

½ cup / 75g sliced (about 2 inches / 5cm) yellow or red bell pepper (about ½ large pepper)

3 tablespoons toasted sesame oil

2 tablespoons rice cooking wine

1 teaspoon ground black pepper

2 tablespoons toasted sesame seeds (page 51), for garnish

1 Place a large pan over high heat and add 1 tablespoon of the vegetable oil. When the oil begins to shimmer, add the onions and carrots and season with a pinch of salt.

2 Sauté the onions and carrots 2 to 3 minutes, then add the green and red cabbages along with the remaining 1 tablespoon vegetable oil and another pinch of salt and cook for about a minute or so to keep the vegetables al dente. Then add the broccoli and cauliflower, along with another pinch of salt. Stir until the vegetables start to soften, 2 to 3 minutes.

3 Create a space in the middle of the pan and add the rice noodles. Add the seasoned soy sauce, garlic, and sugar on top of the noodles and toss to coat the noodles. Mix in the sautéed vegetables, then add the mushrooms, chives, and bell pepper. Continue mixing for 30 seconds, then, while still on high heat, add the sesame oil, cooking wine, and black pepper. Sauté until the liquid evaporates and the sauce is fully absorbed.

4 Transfer the japchae to a large serving bowl or plate and garnish with the sesame seeds. Serve immediately—it's best while it's still hot.

VEGETARIAN, VEGAN

매운 오징어 구이

Spicy BBQ Squid

Serves 6 to 8

This spicy squid can be cooked after just two hours in the marinade, but I recommend letting it sit overnight so it can really absorb all the spicy-sweet flavors. I suggest grilling the squid, but you can also use your broiler or cook the squid on the stovetop. While there are six squid in this recipe, I have found that it can serve up to eight, depending on everyone's appetite and how many banchan and other dishes are being shared at the table.

- 1 cup / 200g granulated sugar
- ¾ cup plus 2 tablespoons / 157g coarse gochugaru
- ¾ cup / 285g gochujang
- ¾ cup / 175ml toasted sesame oil
- ½ cup / 164g light corn syrup
- ¼ cup / 125g Gahreun Mahneul / Blended Garlic (page 49)
- 2 tablespoons soy sauce
- 4 teaspoons Gahreun Senggang / Blended Ginger (page 89)
- 4 teaspoons ground black pepper
- 6 whole squid (5 to 6 lb / 2.3 to 2.7kg), cleaned
- 2 or 3 green onions, green and white parts, chopped, for garnish
- ½ teaspoon toasted sesame seeds (page 51), for garnish

1 Place the sugar, gochugaru, gochujang, sesame oil, corn syrup, garlic, soy sauce, ginger, and black pepper in a large bowl and stir to combine. Add the squid and marinate for at least 2 hours (preferably overnight) in the fridge.

2 When you're ready to cook, preheat a grill to high. When the grill is hot, add the squid and cook, flipping once or twice, until the squid just turns opaque, 3 to 5 minutes. Lay the squid on a serving platter and garnish with the green onions and sesame seeds before serving.

▶▶▶ **You can also use your broiler to cook the squid,** just be careful that the squid doesn't burn, since it will cook very quickly under the high heat. Or, if you prefer to cook the squid on the stovetop, start with a few tablespoons of canola, vegetable, or other neutral oil and make sure the oil is smoking hot before adding the squid.

OJINGEO BOKKEUM

오징어볶음

Spicy Stir-Fried Squid with Vegetables

Serves 4 to 6

This is a quick stir-fry for anyone who loves squid and spice as much as I do. I like to use zucchini and carrots here, but you can also use bell peppers or even cabbage if you prefer. To retain the squid's nice chewy texture, be sure to remove the pan from the heat just as the squid turns white and cooks through; if you overcook it, the squid may become rubbery. When shopping for squid, go to a trusted fishmonger or market counter and seek out the freshest you can find. Fresh squid should be shiny and plump, opaque in color, with a clean ocean scent. You can serve this dish with hot rice or somyeon (somen) noodles to absorb the sauce. You can also add soaked rice cakes with the yellow onions and zucchini, and cook until the rice cakes are tender.

- 2 to 3 lb / 900g to 1.4kg whole squid, cleaned
- 1 medium carrot
- 1 medium zucchini
- 2 tablespoons vegetable or other neutral oil
- 2 tablespoons Gahreun Mahneul / Blended Garlic (page 49)
- ⅔ cup / 158g Maeun Yangnum / Spicy Red Pepper Marinade (page 88)
- 2 tablespoons granulated sugar
- 1 tablespoon coarse gochugaru
- ¼ teaspoon ground black pepper

- 1 large yellow onion, cut into 1-inch / 2.5cm slices
- ½ to 1 jalapeño, sliced (optional)
- 1 tablespoon toasted sesame oil
- 3 to 5 green onions, cut into 2-inch / 5cm slices, green and white parts
- 1 tablespoon toasted sesame seeds (page 51), for garnish

1 Lay the whole squid on a cutting board and score it in several places with a knife. Slice the squid, carrot, and zucchini into pieces about 1 by 2 inches / 2.5 by 5cm and set aside.

2 Place a large sauté pan over high heat and add the vegetable oil. When the oil begins to smoke, lower the heat to medium and add the garlic. Sauté the garlic until fragrant, 30 seconds to 1 minute, then add the squid. Toss to combine, then stir in the red pepper marinade and sugar. Mix to combine, then add the gochugaru and black pepper. Stir until fully incorporated.

3 Increase the heat to high. Add the carrots and stir for 2 to 3 minutes. Add the yellow onions, zucchini, as many slices of jalapeño as you'd like (if using), and 2 tablespoons water and stir. Cook just until the squid turns from translucent to opaque. Add the sesame oil and green onions and stir.

4 Sprinkle the sesame seeds over the pan and remove from the heat. Serve immediately.

SENGSUN JORIM
생선조림

Braised Fish with Radish and Vegetables

Serves 6 to 8

This spicy braise features fresh black cod tucked between several layers of vegetables, and I especially like it as a healthier alternative to frying the fish. The heat that comes from the dadaegi and gochugaru is a perfect complement to the delicate flavor of the cod. Freshness is important here; if black cod isn't available, substitute another fresh fish, like sea bass, cod, mackerel, croaker, or pike. Korean and many Asian markets usually have well-stocked fish counters with many varieties of fresh fish for you to try, and they often will fillet the whole fish for you if requested. If they do, ask the fishmonger to throw in the head, too, as it'll add even more flavor to the braise.

- 1 lb / 450g mu (Korean radish), peeled (about 1 medium radish)
- 1 (3-lb / 1.4kg) black cod fillet (preferably with the head on), cleaned and trimmed
- 1 jalapeño, sliced
- 2 cups / 140g shishito peppers
- 1 medium yellow onion, cut into ½-inch / 12mm slices
- 1 bunch green onions, green and white parts, cut into 2-inch / 5cm pieces
- 1¾ cups / 420g Maeun Yangnum / Spicy Red Pepper Marinade (page 88)
- 1¾ cups / 415ml Mat Ganjang / Seasoned Soy Sauce (page 88)
- 2½ tablespoons Gahreun Mahneul / Blended Garlic (page 49)

- 4½ teaspoons toasted sesame oil
- ½ teaspoon ground black pepper
- ½ teaspoon Gahreun Senggang / Blended Ginger (page 89)
- 1½ teaspoons toasted sesame seeds (page 51), for garnish

1 Slice the radish into pieces ½ inch / 12mm thick by 2 inches / 5cm wide and arrange them in a single layer in a heavy-bottomed pot like a donabe (Japanese clay pot) or Dutch oven.

2 Slice the fish into 2-inch / 5cm pieces and place on top of the radishes. Layer the jalapeño and shishito peppers over the fish. (The shishito peppers should be about 2 inches / 5cm in length; if they're longer, cut them in half.)

3 Next, place the yellow onions on top of the peppers. Finally, layer the green onions on top of the yellow onions.

4 In a large bowl, combine the red pepper marinade, seasoned soy sauce, garlic, sesame oil, black pepper, and ginger with ½ cup / 120ml water. Stir to combine all the ingredients, then pour evenly over the whole pot.

5 Place the pot over high heat and bring to a boil. Cook the fish and vegetables, uncovered, using a large spoon to constantly spoon the liquid over the layered ingredients until the liquid reduces by half and the fish is firm and cooked through, 20 to 30 minutes, depending on the thickness and texture of the fish. Remove the pot from the heat and garnish with the sesame seeds. It's lovely served at the table, right out of the pot.

YANGNYUM GALBI
양념 갈비

LA Galbi

Serves 6 to 8

Galbi, I think, is often undervalued. For many, it's synonymous with all-you-can-eat Korean BBQ, and that association has led to a perception that galbi doesn't take much time to prepare or that lesser-quality meat can be used. But making very good galbi does indeed take time and care, and the quality of the beef does matter. At my restaurant, I always used choice beef, and I do so at home, too. Of course, a higher grade of beef is more costly than lower grades, but the flavor is worth the expense.

I also use LA-style galbi, which are short ribs cut across the bone. Korean and Asian markets often label this cut as LA galbi; you may also see it, especially outside of those markets, labeled as flanken or crosscut short ribs. Once you invest in high-quality galbi, it is worth taking a few extra steps to tenderize the ribs so they don't end up tough and chewy. To do so, I pound the meat with a meat tenderizer, and I include kiwi in the marinade—the kiwi contains acids that break down the meat's proteins, and mashing ensures it will be evenly distributed throughout the marinade. I love cooking galbi on a hot grill, but you can use a heavy skillet (preferably cast-iron) instead. The galbi is served on a bed of sizzling-hot onions, which are seasoned with sesame oil. As the onions sit, they will absorb the flavors of the galbi. Don't overlook them: I promise these will be some of the best onions you've ever had!

10 lb / 4.5kg LA-style galbi, preferably choice or prime grade
1 small kiwi, peeled, mashed, and strained (about 2 tablespoons)
3 cups / 600g granulated sugar
2 cups / 480ml soy sauce
1 cup / 347g light corn syrup
¾ cup / 188g Gahreun Mahneul / Blended Garlic (page 49)
¼ cup plus 2 tablespoons / 90ml toasted sesame oil, plus more for sautéing
1 tablespoon plus ¾ teaspoon ground black pepper
1¼ teaspoons Gahreun Senggang / Blended Ginger (page 89)
½ medium yellow onion, thinly sliced
1 or 2 green onions, green and white parts, chopped, for garnish
½ teaspoon toasted sesame seeds (page 51), for garnish

1 Pound the short ribs with a meat tenderizer. Place the ribs in a large bowl, cover with cold tap water, and soak in the refrigerator for 1 hour. Drain, then refill the bowl with fresh water, and soak the ribs again in the fridge for another hour. After soaking the second time, rinse the ribs and place them in a colander to drain.

2 In a separate large bowl, combine 7 cups / 1.7L cold tap water with the kiwi, sugar, soy sauce, corn syrup, garlic, sesame oil, black pepper, and ginger and mix well. Lay the ribs flat in the marinade, being as gentle as possible so the meat doesn't separate from the bones. Place the ribs in the fridge and marinate for at least 6 hours or, for best results, overnight.

CONTINUED

3 When you're ready to cook, preheat a grill or place a cast-iron skillet over high heat. Once the skillet is hot, add the ribs. Because they're so thin, they will cook quickly, in just a few minutes per side. Remove the ribs and set aside.

4 Place a medium skillet over medium heat. Once the skillet is hot, add a splash of oil and the yellow onions. Sauté until the onions soften and char slightly, a few minutes. Place the onions on a serving platter and lay the ribs on top. Garnish with the green onions and sesame seeds and share immediately with family and friends.

Galbi, LA Style

When I arrived in Los Angeles from Korea in 1977, one of the first places I visited was a Korean market in Koreatown. It was there that I had LA-style galbi for the first time. It was so delicious that I ate over twenty pieces!

I was familiar with galbi, of course, but the galbi I knew was prepared differently from what I ate that day at the market. Classic galbi is made by slicing the short ribs between the bones. A thick piece of meat is left attached to the bone, which is sliced precisely by the butcher or cooked so it unfolds elegantly into one long strip. The entire strip is then marinated and grilled.

Koreans in Los Angeles were making galbi using the same flavors but with a different cut called flanken, which was widely available and was common in Eastern European, Jewish, and Mexican cooking. Here the ribs are sliced thinly across several bones, rather than between them, so each slice of meat has the cross sections of a few bones right along the top. No additional slicing is necessary—it is ready to be used right away.

When Koreans immigrated to Los Angeles, they adopted this cut to make galbi, and it is easy to see why. Sliced thinly, it just takes a few minutes on a grill to cook, so you can feed many people very quickly. It's easy for everyone, from children to seniors, to hold and eat. With less bone, this cut offers more meat per pound, so it is a very economical option. And it is less expensive in terms of time, too, because there is no need to carefully slice and unfold the meat before marinating and grilling. This savings in labor is one likely reason it became popular in restaurants throughout Koreatown.

By the 1980s, the flanken cut became associated with Korean BBQ, and even the *Los Angeles Times* instructed readers to use flanken cuts in their galbi recipes. This style became more generally known as LA galbi across the country. LA galbi has even made it to South Korea, where it's sold in supermarkets and served at restaurants! No matter where you are, then, you will be reminded of Los Angeles when you have LA galbi. In many ways, it reflects LA well: It is the product of the intermingling of the region's many cultures as well as the creative ways in which immigrants have adapted to their circumstances. And it is casual and unfussy—just like Los Angeles!

I served LA galbi at Beverly Soon Tofu, and many customers ordered it along with their soon tofu for a complete meal. That recipe, adapted for the home, is the one I share with you here. Serve it with soon tofu, as I did at my restaurant, or include it as part of a Korean BBQ spread (see Korean BBQ at Home, page 218). LA galbi is also very portable, so marinate it overnight and take it with you to your next picnic, potluck, or any other gathering.

불고기

Bulgogi

Serves 4 to 6

Bulgogi, thin slices of beef flavored in a soy sauce–based marinade, is an extremely versatile dish. It's delicious served with steamed rice and banchan, for example, or it can be tossed with your bibimbap or even added to a Bulgogi Jeongol (page 210). Kids and parents alike love how tender the meat is and how easy it is to eat. Because bulgogi uses a less-expensive cut of beef than, say, galbi, it's also an affordable option if you need to serve a large crowd. That said, look for choice, prime, or the highest-quality beef within your budget. Lower grades of beef tend to be fatty and lack a good beefy flavor. If you want to slice the meat yourself, freeze the beef for about an hour, then remove and slice the meat thinly across the grain. Alternatively, some butchers will slice the meat for you, and many Asian markets sell pre-sliced beef specifically intended to be cooked as bulgogi. These days, Costco sells sliced rib eye, too!

For best results, marinate the beef overnight and cook it over a hot grill the next day. If you don't have a grill, a broiler will also work, or you can certainly cook the slices in an oiled pan on the stovetop.

- 4 lb / 1.8kg rib eye, chuck roll, or boneless short ribs, sliced
- ½ medium yellow onion, thinly sliced
- 1 cup / 240ml soy sauce
- 1 cup / 200g granulated sugar
- ¼ cup / 63g Gahreun Mahneul / Blended Garlic (page 49)
- ¼ cup / 82g light corn syrup
- 1 small kiwi, peeled, mashed, and strained (about 2 tablespoons)
- 2 tablespoons toasted sesame oil
- 1½ teaspoons ground black pepper
- ½ teaspoon Gahreun Senggang / Blended Ginger (page 89)
- 1 or 2 green onions, green and white parts, chopped, for garnish
- ½ teaspoon toasted sesame seeds (page 51), for garnish

1 Place the beef in a large bowl, cover with cold tap water, and soak in the refrigerator for at least 2 hours. Then drain, rinse, and soak the beef for another 2 hours in the fridge. Pour the beef into a colander, rinse, and drain one more time.

2 In a separate large bowl, combine 1 cup / 240ml water with the yellow onions, soy sauce, sugar, garlic, corn syrup, kiwi, sesame oil, black pepper, and ginger and mix well. Gently add the beef to the marinade, laying the slices flat to ensure the marinade is as evenly distributed as possible. Place the bowl in the refrigerator and marinate at least 3 hours, preferably overnight.

3 When you're ready to cook, preheat a grill to high. Working in batches to avoid over-crowding, grill the beef until cooked through, just a few minutes per side. Garnish with the green onions and sesame seeds and serve.

MAEUN YANGNYUM DAEJI GALBI JJIM
매운양념돼지갈비찜

Braised Spicy Pork Ribs

Serves 4

This dish takes pork ribs to another level. It's a centerpiece dish, perfect for entertaining because you can make it ahead of time and complement it with plenty of appetizers and banchan. In total, the ribs will braise for about two hours, during which time the meat will become fall-off-the-bone tender. The braising liquid has multiple levels of spice, thanks to the gochujang, gochugaru, and jalapeños, all of which will no doubt make you and your guests thirsty for a cold shot of soju or a refreshing cup of makgeolli.

- 4 lb / 1.8kg pork spareribs
- 1½ cups / 360ml orange juice
- 2 or 3 jalapeños, sliced
- ½ cup / 120ml soju
- ¼ cup plus 2 tablespoons / 75g granulated sugar
- ¼ cup plus 1 tablespoon / 56g coarse gochugaru
- ¼ cup / 80g Dadaegi / Seasoned Red Pepper Paste (page 49)
- ¼ cup / 60ml Mat Ganjang / Seasoned Soy Sauce (page 88)
- 3 tablespoons Gahreun Mahneul / Blended Garlic (page 49)
- 2 tablespoons gochujang
- 4½ teaspoons toasted sesame oil
- 1½ teaspoons Gahreun Senggang / Blended Ginger (page 89)
- 1½ teaspoons ground black pepper
- 1 medium yellow onion, sliced
- 6 green onions, sliced into 4 to 6 segments, plus 1, chopped, for garnish
- 1 tablespoon toasted sesame seeds (page 51)

1 Slice the pork between the bones into individual ribs, then score the ribs by making several shallow cuts across the surface of each.

2 In a large bowl, combine the ribs and orange juice, then add enough cold tap water to cover the ribs completely. Set the bowl aside for at least 2 hours, then drain and rinse the ribs (if setting aside for longer than 2 hours, transfer the ribs to the refrigerator).

3 In a separate large bowl, combine 2½ cups / 590ml water with the jalapeños, soju, sugar, gochugaru, dadaegi, seasoned soy sauce, garlic, gochujang, 1 tablespoon of the sesame oil, the ginger, and black pepper. Mix well.

4 Place a large pot over high heat and add the ribs and spice mixture. If the liquid doesn't cover the ribs, add enough water, up to ½ cup / 120ml, to submerge the ribs. Boil until the liquid reduces by at least half, 30 to 40 minutes, stirring and spooning the liquid over the ribs frequently as it boils. As you do so, skim the fat that rises to the top.

5 When the liquid reduces by at least half, lower the heat to medium and simmer for 1½ hours, frequently spooning the braising liquid over the ribs.

6 Add the yellow and green onion segments and cook until the onions and ribs are tender, 5 to 10 minutes. Add the remaining 1½ teaspoons oil and sprinkle in the sesame seeds. Transfer the ribs, and their delicious braising liquid, to a large serving bowl, garnish with the sliced green onions, and serve.

YANGNYUM DAEJI GALBI GUI

양념돼지갈비구이

Soy-Marinated BBQ Pork Ribs

Serves 4

Contrary to popular perception, not all Korean pork dishes are spicy. These pork spareribs are an excellent example: they're sweet, sticky, charred, and meaty, and while there is a jalapeño in the marinade, the pepper imparts more flavor than heat. Plan to marinate the ribs for at least a few hours (ideally, overnight) before cooking, so the ribs can absorb as much of the soy sauce marinade as possible. After that, it's a quick three-step process to make the ribs. You'll first partially cook the ribs in their own marinade, then sear them on a grill before returning them to the pot until they're very tender. While the ribs aren't on the grill very long, that step is worth the time: the char and smokiness you gain are irreplaceable.

- 4 lb / 1.8kg pork spareribs
- 1½ cups / 360ml orange juice
- 1 cup / 240ml Mat Ganjang / Seasoned Soy Sauce (page 88)
- ½ cup / 120ml soju
- ¼ cup / 50g granulated sugar
- 3 tablespoons Gahreun Mahneul / Blended Garlic (page 49)
- 1½ teaspoons Gahreun Senggang / Blended Ginger (page 89)
- 1 teaspoon ground black pepper
- 1 medium yellow onion, sliced into 8 wedges
- 1 jalapeño, sliced
- 4 green onions, sliced, plus 1, chopped, for garnish
- 1 tablespoon toasted sesame oil
- 2 tablespoons toasted sesame seeds (page 51), for garnish

1 Cut the pork between the bones into individual ribs, then make several shallow cuts across the surface of each rib.

2 In a large bowl, combine the ribs and orange juice, then add enough cold tap water to cover the ribs completely. Set the bowl aside for at least 2 hours, then drain and rinse the ribs (if setting aside for longer than 2 hours, transfer the ribs to the refrigerator).

3 In a separate large bowl, combine 2 cups / 480ml water with the seasoned soy sauce, soju, sugar, garlic, ginger, and black pepper. Mix well. Add the ribs, yellow onions, and jalapeños and coat the ribs with the marinade. Marinate in the refrigerator for at least 5 hours, preferably overnight.

4 Place a large pot over high heat and add the ribs and marinating liquid. The liquid should cover the ribs; if it doesn't, add enough water, up to ½ cup / 120ml, to submerge the ribs. Boil, uncovered, for 35 minutes. The liquid will thicken into a sauce as it boils. Turn down the heat to low and simmer for an additional 20 minutes.

5 While the ribs are simmering, preheat a grill to high.

6 Just as you're about done simmering, place the sliced green onions in a small bowl. Add the sesame oil and stir. Add the mixture to the pot and cover for 5 to 10 minutes.

7 Keeping the pot at a simmer, remove the ribs and place them on the grill. Sear them until both sides are caramelized, not more than a minute or two on each side. Transfer the grilled ribs back to the pot, cover, and cook on low heat for another 15 to 20 minutes, or until the ribs are tender.

8 Place the ribs on a serving platter, spoon the sauce over them, and garnish with the chopped green onion and sesame seeds. Serve.

DAKDORITANG
닭도리탕
Spicy Braised Chicken

Serves 4

Braised in Maeun Yangnum / Spicy Red Pepper Marinade (page 88) and garlic, this chicken is perfect for a small dinner or a party. I prefer to use the smaller Jidori chicken for its fresh and tender taste, but if it is not available, any small chicken will do. I also like to break down a whole chicken myself so I have the bones to make broth later, but you can use any combination of chicken parts you prefer. If you have a portable burner, you can finish the braise right at the table, so the chicken stays warm while everyone helps themselves. And don't forget the drinks: this dish is great with cold beer.

- 1 (3-lb / 1.4kg) whole chicken, or 3 lb / 1.4kg chicken parts
- 1 cup / 240g Maeun Yangnum / Spicy Red Pepper Marinade (page 88)
- 2 tablespoons coarse gochugaru
- 2 tablespoons Gahreun Mahneul / Blended Garlic (page 49)
- 4½ teaspoons toasted sesame oil
- ¼ teaspoon Gahreun Senggang / Blended Ginger (page 89)

- ¼ teaspoon ground black pepper
- 1 medium carrot, cut into 1-inch / 2.5cm pieces
- 1 or 2 jalapeños, sliced
- 1 medium yellow onion, sliced into 2-inch / 5cm pieces
- 2 tablespoons light corn syrup
- 3 or 4 green onions, green and white parts, sliced into 2-inch / 5cm pieces

JIDORI CHICKEN

Jidori chickens are free-range chickens originally bred in Japan and now raised on farms across California. Fed a vegetarian diet free of antibiotics and hormones, they are minimally processed and, at least here in Los Angeles, delivered to markets within a day of slaughter. As a result, the chicken is exceptionally fresh and flavorful.

1 If using a whole chicken, break it down so you have two wings, two legs, two thighs, and two breasts. Remove most of the skin from all the pieces and discard or reserve for another use. Slice the thighs and breasts into 2-inch / 5cm pieces, then deeply score all the pieces of chicken in a few different places with a knife to ensure they will fully absorb all the flavors of the broth. Place the pieces in a large bowl and set aside.

2 In a separate large bowl, combine the red pepper marinade, gochugaru, garlic, 1 tablespoon of the sesame oil, the ginger, black pepper, and ¼ cup / 60ml water. Mix well. Pour the marinade over the chicken and place in the refrigerator to marinate for at least 6 hours, preferably overnight.

CONTINUED

3 Place a large shallow pan like a wok or cast-iron skillet over high heat and add the marinated chicken, carrots, and jalapeños along with ½ cup / 120ml water. Boil for 10 to 15 minutes. Add another ½ cup / 120ml water and the yellow onions and stir well. Boil until the chicken is cooked through, another 10 to 15 minutes. Turn off the heat, add the corn syrup and the remaining 1½ teaspoons oil, and stir. Garnish with the green onions, transfer to a platter, and serve.

SPINOFF

When you are done with the chicken, save the sauce and any leftover vegetables to make fried rice. Place the braising sauce and vegetables in a large pan or wok set over high heat and add some cooked rice, chopped green onions, and a splash of sesame oil. Sauté until hot. Top with seaweed and a fried egg.

BULGOGI JEONGOL
불고기 전골

Rib Eye Hot Pot

Serves 4

Many cultures have a long history of hot pot, where groups gather around to share a communal pot of soup. That is certainly true in Korea. It's said that the name of our hot pot, jeongol, comes from ancient times, when soldiers, often lacking cooking vessels, would just flip over their helmets and use them to cook their soup. And while jeongol had humble roots, for a time, it was part of the royal table, loaded with expensive meats and vegetables. These days, of course, everyone can enjoy jeongol with family and friends. I often make jeongol during the winter, when the hot soup will warm you up on a cold night. This version uses my bulgogi, but instead of grilling the beef slices, I cook them in the seasoned broth. To complement the bulgogi, I add all sorts of winter vegetables, like bok choy and green cabbage, as well as earthy mushrooms. Of course, you can choose any other seasonal vegetables you'd like. I also like to add rice noodles, but you can use udon, mung bean noodles, glass noodles, or, really, any other noodle to soak up all that delicious broth. As hot pot is a shared dish, I like to cook it right at the table, in a braiser placed over a portable butane burner. The soup should be kept at a gentle simmer so it stays hot throughout the meal. If you don't have a braiser, any wide, shallow pot, or a donabe (Japanese clay pot) will work. And if you don't have a portable burner, setting the pot on the stovetop will work, too.

1   (8-oz / 225g) package dried rice noodles

2   cups / 100g sliced (about 2 inches / 5cm) green or napa cabbage (about ½ medium head)

1   lb / 450g mushrooms (a combination of shiitake, brown or white beech, enoki, and trumpet), torn into 1-inch / 2.5cm pieces

1   cup / 120g sliced yellow onions (about ½ medium onion)

1   lb / 450g bok choy, cored if large, trimmed, washed well, and sliced into bite-sized pieces

2   green onions, green and white parts, sliced into 2-inch / 5cm pieces

4   cups / 950ml homemade beef broth (page 42 or 44) or store-bought, or water, plus more to taste

4½ teaspoons Gahreun Mahneul / Blended Garlic (page 49)

1½ teaspoons fish sauce, plus more to taste

½   teaspoon ground black pepper

1   (19-oz / 538g) package firm tofu, preferably House Foods brand, drained and diced

2   tablespoons soy sauce, plus more to taste

1¾ lb / 790g marinated Bulgogi (page 205)

1 Place the noodles in a large bowl and cover with water. Set aside to soak as you prepare the hot pot.

2 Arrange the cabbage, mushrooms, yellow onions, bok choy, and green onions in a braiser or other wide, shallow pot. Pour in the beef broth, then add the garlic, fish sauce, and black pepper. Add the tofu and pour the soy sauce directly over the tofu pieces so they can absorb some of the seasoning.

3 Once all the vegetables and tofu are arranged, place the pot over high heat. When it begins to boil, reduce the heat to low, add the drained noodles, and slowly simmer until everything is cooked, 3 to 5 minutes. Add the bulgogi to the center of the pot and cook until the meat is just cooked through, a few minutes.

4 Taste and add more broth if you'd like. You can also season the pot with a splash or two more of fish sauce or soy sauce. If you have prepared the hot pot on a portable butane burner at the table, lower the heat to a bare simmer so the pot will stay warm throughout the meal. Otherwise, place it on a trivet at the table and enjoy the hot pot together with your party.

SOOYOOK
수육

Slow-Cooked Brisket

Serves 8 to 10

If you've ever had sullungtang (bone broth) at a Koreatown restaurant in Los Angeles, you probably are familiar with sooyook, or the brisket often served with the broth. It's a large dish that's great to share. I often prepare this for large crowds and serve it alongside a delicious dipping sauce made with my Mat Ganjang / Seasoned Soy Sauce (page 89) and plenty of side dishes, like Spicy Cucumbers (page 94). The broth includes whole untrimmed green onions; I like to keep the roots because they are sweet and full of nutrients. They are also the most fragrant part of the vegetable, which helps neutralize any

CONTINUED

gamy smell from the brisket, as do the chiles. I use Chinese dried red chiles, which are usually not much more than 3 to 4 inches / 7.5 to 10cm in length and are often labeled simply as dried red peppers at Asian markets.

If you're planning ahead, this whole dish can easily be prepared ahead of time. You can begin cooking 2 to 2½ hours before the party starts. Once your guests arrive, the brisket will be just about ready to be sliced and served.

Brisket

8	lb / 3.6kg beef brisket, trimmed
12	whole black peppercorns
10	to 12 garlic cloves
2	or 3 whole dried red chile peppers, or 1 jalapeño, halved
1	tablespoon soy sauce
3	or 4 bunches green onions, roots untrimmed
1	medium yellow onion, unpeeled, quartered
1	cup / 240ml rice cooking wine

Dipping Sauce

½	bunch green onions, chopped green onions, green and white parts
¼	cup / 60ml Mat Ganjang / Seasoned Soy Sauce (page 88)
1	teaspoon wasabi, plus more to taste
1	teaspoon white vinegar
1	teaspoon rice cooking wine

TO PREPARE THE BRISKET

1 Slice the brisket into pieces 6 to 8 inches / 15 to 20cm in length (if not already pre-sliced by a butcher). Place the brisket in a large bowl (or two large bowls if necessary), cover with cold tap water, and soak in the refrigerator for 2 hours.

2 Place a large stockpot over high heat and add 5 qt / 4.7L water. Once the water is boiling, add the peppercorns, garlic cloves, chile peppers, and soy sauce and continue to boil for 15 to 20 minutes. Add the drained brisket and green and yellow onions and continue to boil over high heat, periodically skimming the fat and impurities that rise to the surface with a slotted spoon or ladle. After about 1½ hours, add the cooking wine to the pot and continue to boil for 30 minutes more. Insert a chopstick into the brisket; if the chopstick easily pierces the meat, the brisket is ready. If it's not yet tender enough, continue to boil for another 5 to 10 minutes, then check again. The total cooking time for the brisket should be 2 to 2½ hours, depending on the thickness of the beef.

TO MAKE THE DIPPING SAUCE

3 While the brisket is cooking, place the green onions, seasoned soy sauce, wasabi, vinegar, and cooking wine in a medium bowl. Mix and set aside.

4 Once the brisket is cooked, remove the pieces from the pot and set aside to cool for 15 minutes. It is important to allow the brisket to cool before slicing. If you slice too early, you'll tear the meat and its juices will escape, resulting in tough, chewy pieces. If you'd like even more broth with your meat, add 4 cups / 950ml water to the broth in the pot and boil for 30 to 40 minutes.

5 Strain the broth into a large container and discard the solids. When you're ready to serve, slice the meat against the grain (slicing the meat this way will result in tender pieces that will be easier to eat) and fan out the slices on a serving platter. Pour the strained broth over the slices and offer your guests their own bowls of sauce to dip their brisket into as they wish.

YANGNYUM DAKGOGI GUI
양념 닭고기 구이

Soy-Marinated BBQ Chicken

Serves 4 to 6

If you like the flavors of bulgogi but would prefer chicken rather than beef, the marinade for this chicken will do the trick. It doesn't have any spicy components in it either, so it's a great option for those who want a milder BBQ dish. The marinated chicken is best cooked on a grill, but I also include directions to cook the chicken on the stovetop if you prefer.

- **2 lb / 900g boneless, skinless chicken thighs or breasts**
- **½ cup / 120ml soy sauce**
- **½ cup / 100g granulated sugar**
- **2 tablespoons Gahreun Mahneul / Blended Garlic (page 49)**
- **2 tablespoons light corn syrup**
- **2 tablespoons rice cooking wine**
- **1 tablespoon toasted sesame oil**
- **¾ teaspoon ground black pepper**
- **½ teaspoon Gahreun Senggang / Blended Ginger (page 89)**
  Vegetable oil, for the grill

1 In a large bowl, combine 1 cup / 240ml water, the soy sauce, sugar, garlic, corn syrup, cooking wine, sesame oil, black pepper, and ginger and stir well to make the marinade.

2 If using breasts, place one breast on a cutting board. With your palm flat on top of the breast, slice the chicken in half horizontally with a sharp knife so you end up with two thin fillets. Repeat with the remaining chicken breasts.

3 Add the chicken pieces to the bowl. Using your hands, coat the chicken evenly in the marinade. Transfer the bowl to the refrigerator and marinate for at least 5 hours, preferably overnight.

4 When you're ready to cook, preheat a grill to high. When it's hot, lightly oil the grill add the chicken pieces. Cook until they're cooked through (the temperature should read 165°F / 75°C on a meat thermometer) and begin to caramelize, 4 to 6 minutes on each side, depending on the thickness of the pieces and the temperature of the grill. Serve.

▶▶▶ **If you prefer to cook the chicken on the stovetop,** lightly oil a large skillet with vegetable oil and place it over medium heat. Once the oil begins to smoke, use tongs to pull the chicken out of the marinade and place in the pan. Brown the chicken on both sides, then reduce the heat to low and cook until done, about 8-12 minutes.

매운 닭고기 구이

Spicy BBQ Chicken

Serves 4

This spicy grilled chicken is perfect served with hot rice, alongside a nice salad, or stuffed into a sandwich for a quick and satisfying lunch. You can marinate the chicken for as little as just a few hours, but for the very best results, marinate the chicken the night before you plan to grill it so the pieces can really soak up all the spicy-salty-sweet flavors of the marinade.

- ¾ cup / 135g coarse gochugaru
- ½ cup / 100g granulated sugar
- ¼ cup / 60ml soy sauce
- ¼ cup / 95g gochujang
- ¼ cup / 80g Dadaegi / Seasoned Red Pepper Paste (page 49)
- 3 tablespoons light corn syrup
- 2 tablespoons Gahreun Mahneul / Blended Garlic (page 49)
- 2 tablespoons toasted sesame oil
- 1½ teaspoons ground black pepper
- ¾ teaspoon Gahreun Senggang / Blended Ginger (page 89)
- 3 lb / 1.4kg boneless, skinless chicken thighs or breast
  Vegetable or other neutral oil, for the grill
  Sliced green onions, for garnish
  Toasted sesame seeds, for garnish
  (page 51)

1 In a large bowl, combine 1¾ cups / 415ml water, the gochugaru, sugar, soy sauce, gochujang, dadaegi, corn syrup, garlic, sesame oil, black pepper, and ginger. Stir until the ingredients are well combined and set aside.

2 If using breasts, place one breast on a cutting board. With your palm flat on top of the breast, slice the chicken in half horizontally with a sharp knife so you end up with two thin fillets. Repeat with the remaining chicken breasts.

3 Add the chicken pieces to the bowl. Using your hands, coat the chicken evenly in the marinade. Transfer the bowl to the refrigerator and marinate for at least 5 hours, preferably overnight.

4 When you're ready to cook, lightly oil a grill and preheat to medium-high. When the grill is hot, add the chicken pieces and grill until they're nicely charred and halfway cooked, just a few minutes, then flip and grill until the juices run clear and the chicken is cooked through (the temperature should read 165°F / 75°C on a meat thermometer), 20 to 30 minutes total.

5 Transfer the chicken to a large platter and garnish with the green onions and sesame seeds before serving.

▸▸▸ **If you prefer to cook the chicken on the stovetop,** lightly oil a large skillet with vegetable oil and place it over medium heat. Once the oil begins to smoke, use tongs to pull the chicken out of the marinade and place in the pan. Brown the chicken on both sides, then reduce the heat to low and cook until done, about 8-12 minutes.

MAEUN DAEJI BULGOGI

매운 돼지 불고기

Spicy BBQ Pork

Serves 4

This is always one of the most popular items at my BBQ parties. I love the combination of pork shoulder and belly, but if you'd prefer less fat, use only pork shoulder. For convenience, Korean and many other Asian markets sell pre-sliced pork in their meat departments. For best results, plan ahead: you'll need a few hours to soak the meat before it goes into the marinade, then you'll want to marinate it overnight to allow the pork to absorb all the spicy-sweet flavors. If you grill the pork, as I do here, be sure the heat on the grill is evenly distributed; otherwise, you may burn the marinade while undercooking the meat. Alternatively, cook the pork on your stovetop using an oiled pan set over medium-high heat and add the pork once the oil is smoking hot so the pork will sear nicely rather than steam in its liquid. Either way you cook it, I highly suggest having a stack of cold, crisp lettuce leaves ready, too, as they make excellent wrappers—and they will cool you and your taste buds down from the spicy pork!

3 to 4 lb / 1.4 to 1.8kg pork shoulder, pork belly, or a combination of both, thinly sliced

2 or 3 slices jalapeño

¼ cup plus 2 tablespoons / 68g coarse gochugaru

¼ cup plus 1 tablespoon / 63g granulated sugar

¼ cup plus 1 tablespoon / 75ml toasted sesame oil, plus more for sautéing

¼ cup plus 1 tablespoon / 103g light corn syrup

¼ cup / 60ml Mat Ganjang / Seasoned Soy Sauce (page 88)

¼ cup / 60ml rice cooking wine

3 tablespoons gochujang

3 tablespoons Gahreun Mahneul / Blended Garlic (page 49)

2 tablespoons Dadaegi / Seasoned Red Pepper Paste (page 49)

1 tablespoon fish sauce

1½ teaspoons Gahreun Senggang / Blended Ginger (page 89)

1 teaspoon ground black pepper

1 medium yellow onion, thinly sliced

5 green onions, green and white parts, chopped, for garnish

1 or 2 heads red or green leaf lettuce, leaves separated, then washed and dried completely, for serving (optional)

1 To remove the residual impurities and congealed blood in the meat, soak the pork in cold tap water for at least 2 hours in the fridge. Rinse with cold water, soak for another 2 hours, then rinse one final time. Place the pork in a colander set over a bowl to drain.

2 While the pork drains, combine the jalapeño, gochugaru, sugar, sesame oil, corn syrup, seasoned soy sauce, cooking wine, gochujang, garlic, dadaegi, fish sauce, ginger, and black pepper with 1 cup / 240ml water in a large bowl. Mix well. Add the pork and submerge it in the marinade. Place the bowl in the refrigerator and marinate the pork for at least 4 hours, preferably overnight.

3 When you're ready to cook, preheat a grill to high. Once the grill is hot, grill the pork until cooked through, just a few minutes per side. Work in batches as necessary to avoid crowding the grill. Set aside.

4 Place a medium skillet over medium heat. Once the pan is hot, add a splash of oil and the yellow onions. Sauté the onions until they soften and are charred a bit at the edges, just a few minutes. Place the onions on a large dish or other serving platter and add the ribs on top. Garnish with the green onions. If serving the pork with lettuce leaves, encourage guests to wrap the lettuce around a few slices of pork and some onions for a delicious bite.

Korean BBQ at Home

Making Korean BBQ at home is easier than ever. All you need is a grill pan, a portable butane burner, and a few canisters of fuel so you can grill right at the table. You can find grill pans for Korean BBQ at Asian markets and online; these grill pans include drip trays and separate sections to keep cooked meats warm. I recommend grill pans made of cast iron; if properly seasoned, they will last forever.

As for the menu, I've included a few ideas here; many of these items can be prepared ahead of time. And don't forget the drinks: nothing beats ice-cold soju with BBQ.

Meat and Vegetables

The night before your meal, marinate any or all of the following:

- **LA Galbi** (page 200)
- **Bulgogi** (page 205)
- **Yangnyum Dakgogi Gui** / Soy-Marinated BBQ Chicken (page 213)

If you or your guests like spicy food, the following are great options as well:

- **Maeun Daeji Bulgogi** / Spicy BBQ Pork (page 216)
- **Maeun Ojingeo Gui** / Spicy BBQ Squid (page 197)

The day of your party, slice some kabocha squash, onions, and mushrooms. They will be delicious when grilled, too.

Banchan, Appetizers, and Other Small Dishes to Have on the Side

These banchan are all great with grilled meats:

- **Oh Eeh Muchim** / Sweet and Tangy Cucumbers (page 93) or **Maeun Oh Eeh Muchim** / Spicy Cucumbers (pages 94)
- **Mu Saeng Chae** / Matchstick Radishes (page 90)
- **Gamja Bokkeum** / Sautéed Shoestring Potatoes (page 105)
- **Kongnamul** / Soybean Sprouts (page 91)
- **Gyeran Mari** / Rolled Omelet (page 110)
- **Eomuk Jorim** / Soy-Braised Fish Cakes (page 121)
- **Broccoli Dooboo Muchim** / Broccoli with Tofu (page 97)
- **Kimchi Jeon** / Kimchi Pancakes (page 164)
- **Nokdoo Bindaedduk** / Mung Bean Pancakes (page 160)

Rice

Of course, I like to have **plenty of steamed rice** to eat with the meat!

I also love having the **Minari Salad with Soy Sauce Vinaigrette** (page 176) with **Korean BBQ**. You can prepare the greens and make the dressing ahead of time; just be sure to store the greens separately from the vinaigrette and dress the salad right before serving.

Have a stack of **kkaetnip (perilla leaves) and/ or crisp red or green lettuce leaves** on the table, too—they make excellent wrappers. Prepare a few bowls of **gochujang and doenjang** (fermented soybean paste); these are excellent condiments that can be used as a dip or a spread.

Finally, **slice some cucumbers, garlic cloves, jalapeños, and Korean green chili peppers** for the table.

Kimchi

Kimchi will help cut through the richness of all the meat on the table. Any of my kimchi recipes will complement the meal well. Most people love the classic **Mak Kimchi** (page 129) or, if you have it ready, **Tongbaechoo Kimchi / Spicy Napa Cabbage Kimchi** (page 130).

Alternatively, the **Bok Choy Kimchi** (page 148) and the **Yangpa Kimchi / Yellow Onion Kimchi** (page 152) are good options, and they have the advantage of being quick to make.

Fried Rice and Soups

This is the best part: after everyone has had their fill of BBQ, the **leftovers will make an amazing fried rice.** Place a grill pan or wok on the burner and add all of the remaining banchan. Using scissors, snip the kimchi and meat into bite-sized pieces into the pan, then add the rice, toasted sesame oil to taste, and, if you have it, as much **Maeun Yangnum / Spicy Red Pepper Marinade** (page 88) as you'd like. Add some **seasoned seaweed or furikake** and mix to combine. Let the rice sit until it gets crispy, then serve.

I like to pair this fried rice with my **Kongnamul Guk / Soybean Sprout Soup** (page 225), which is a delicious and light way to end the meal, or with a stew like **Doenjang Soon Tofu / Soybean Paste Soon Tofu** (page 75) or **Gochujang Chigae / Red Pepper Paste Stew with Tofu** (page 224).

Stews and Soups

No meal feels complete to me without a bowl of soup. I tend to make one of two types of soup: a chigae or a guk. Chigaes are stews with thick, hearty broths. They're usually filled with a variety of vegetables and proteins, though the name of the stew tends to indicate its primary ingredient. You already are very familiar with at least one chigae: soon tofu chigae!

Guks are the other kind of soup I like to make. These soups generally are more spare than chigaes; the emphasis is more on the broth than on the fillings. They are especially nourishing and restorative.

The soups and stews here are all part of my regular rotation. They span from comforting guks for cold days to stews as lively and vibrant as a rambunctious dinner party. Whether you serve a soup or a stew, be sure to serve it with rice, one or more banchan (see page 87), and kimchi (see page 123). And, if you'd like, add on any of the larger platters in this book (see page 175); the soups and stews here all complement those shared dishes nicely.

KIMCHI CHIGAE
김치 찌개

Kimchi Stew

Serves 4

If you have kimchi in your fridge, you have
a meal. Once kimchi ferments past its peak
ripeness and becomes too fermented and sour
to eat on its own, I make kimchi chigae, a spicy,
lively stew perfect to warm you up on a cold
night (ripe kimchi can be used, too, though its
sweetness, nuances, and crunch will likely be
lost in the stew). I add pork belly here because it
gives the chigae a rich flavor and velvety texture
that is perfect with hot rice. If you prefer, you
can substitute the pork with just about any
protein you'd like. Some people even like to add
Spam; if you decide to do so, there is no need to
marinate it before adding it to the stew.

- 1 **tablespoon Gahreun Mahneul /
  Blended Garlic (page 49)**
- 1 **tablespoon granulated sugar**
- 1 **tablespoon plus 1 teaspoon toasted
  sesame oil**
- 1 **teaspoon fish sauce**
- ½ **teaspoon Gahreun Senggang /
  Blended Ginger (page 89)**
- ¼ **teaspoon ground black pepper**
- 1 **lb / 450g pork belly, diced into 1-inch /
  2.5cm cubes**
- 4 **cups / 600g chopped kimchi,
  preferably overripened, plus 1 cup /
  240ml kimchi brine**
- ½ **jalapeño, sliced, plus more to taste
  (optional)**
- 1 **tablespoon vegetable or other
  neutral oil**

1 In a large bowl, combine the garlic, sugar,
1 tablespoon of the sesame oil, the fish sauce,
ginger, and black pepper. Add the pork and
marinate for about 15 minutes.

2 In a large stockpot, combine the marinated
pork, kimchi, jalapeño (if using), and vegetable
oil. Stir, then add the kimchi brine and 4 cups
/ 950ml water. Cover the pot and bring the
mixture to a boil. Cook on high heat for about
30 minutes. Turn down the heat to low and
remove the lid to check on the chigae: if you'd
like more broth, add another cup / 240ml
water. Stir to combine the ingredients and
prevent the mixture from burning.

3 Replace the lid and continue to cook at a
simmer for 1 to 1½ hours, depending on how
much broth you'd like. The longer you simmer,
the less broth you'll have, since the kimchi will
absorb more of the liquid and its flavors. Taste
the chigae. If you'd like it even spicier, add
a few more slices of the jalapeño. When the
chigae is to your liking, turn off the heat, add
the remaining 1 teaspoon sesame oil, and serve
with hot rice.

GLUTEN-FREE IF USING GLUTEN-FREE FISH SAUCE

GOCHUJANG CHIGAE
고추장 찌개

Red Pepper Paste Stew with Tofu

Serves 4 to 6

Chigae is often considered a sidekick to a platter of Korean BBQ or another, larger main dish. But this stew can stand alone. It needs little more than hot steamed rice and some kimchi to become a complete meal. And with plenty of chiles, hearty vegetables, and tofu, it's perfect for anyone who loves spicy and savory flavors. To ensure even cooking, dice the vegetables so they are all the same size. I use water to make the broth, but if you have either of my homemade beef broths (pages 42 and 44) in your freezer or refrigerator, feel free to use that instead. Like most stews, the flavors of this chigae will only deepen with time, so it will taste even better the next day.

- 4 oz / 115g short rib trimmings or any other fatty cut of beef
- ½ cup / 124g diced potatoes (about ½ medium russet potato or 2 small red potatoes)
- 3 tablespoons gochujang
- 2 tablespoons Dadaegi / Seasoned Red Pepper Paste (page 49)
- 1 tablespoon Gahreun Mahneul / Blended Garlic (page 49)
- 1 tablespoon coarse gochugaru
- ½ teaspoon toasted sesame oil
- ¼ teaspoon ground black pepper
- ½ cup / 70g chopped yellow onions (about 1 medium onion)
- ½ cup / 60g diced zucchini (about ½ medium zucchini)
- ½ cup / 30g trumpet or oyster mushrooms, chopped
- 1 (19-oz / 538g) package medium or firm tofu, preferably House Foods brand, diced into 1-inch / 2.5cm cubes
- 1 tablespoon fish sauce, plus more to taste
- 2 or 3 slices jalapeño
- 3 or 4 green onions, green and white parts, sliced

1 Place a large stockpot over high heat and add the beef, potatoes, gochujang, dadaegi, garlic, gochugaru, sesame oil, and black pepper. Sauté for a few minutes, then add ½ cup / 120ml water and stir to prevent the ingredients from scorching. Continue to sauté as you bring the water to a boil.

2 Boil until the potatoes are tender, then add the yellow onions, zucchini, and mushrooms and stir. Add 4 cups / 950ml water and continue to cook, undisturbed, until the zucchini is tender, 8 to 10 minutes, then add the tofu, fish sauce, and jalapeño and return to a boil.

3 Add the green onions and continue to boil for another 2 to 3 minutes. Taste the soup and adjust the seasoning, adding more fish sauce as needed. Ladle the stew into individual soup bowls, taking care that each bowl gets a little bit of everythingg.

콩나물국

Soybean Sprout Soup

Serves 4

Winters in Korea are very, very cold, and that's exactly the time you'll find this soup boiling on the stove. Los Angeles doesn't get as chilly, but still, when the weather here turns crisp or when someone has a cold or the flu, I make this soup. It's a simple one to prepare, especially if you always have soybean sprouts in your fridge, as most Korean households do. This is best made with an anchovy and dashi broth; as you cook, you're looking for the sprouts to soften just enough to lose their crispness and no more (if you go much further and overcook it, the broth will become overly fishy in flavor). If you don't have the broth on hand, water is the best substitute. Avoid using beef or chicken broth, since it will overwhelm the delicate flavor of the sprouts. The fish sauce brings a bit of extra umami, but if you don't have any, you can omit it—just give the soup a taste and add a pinch or two more salt, if necessary, before serving.

- 8 cups / 1.9L Anchovy and Dashi Broth (page 48) or store-bought
- 2 cups / 160g soybean sprouts, rinsed
- 1 cup / 120g thinly sliced yellow onions (about 1 medium onion)
- 2 tablespoons Gahreun Mahneul / Blended Garlic (page 49)
- 1 teaspoon sea salt, plus more to taste
- 1 teaspoon fish sauce
- ¼ teaspoon ground black pepper
- 2 or 3 thin slices jalapeño (optional)
- 2 or 3 green onions, green and white parts, sliced, for garnish

1 Place a medium pot over high heat and add the broth, sprouts, yellow onions, garlic, and salt. Once it's boiling, add the fish sauce, black pepper, and jalapeño (if using) and continue to boil. After 5 minutes, taste a sprout (carefully—it will be hot!) to see if it's cooked through: it should be soft and not crisp. If it's not yet cooked, continue boiling for another minute, then check again. Taste the broth and add more salt if needed.

2 Pour the soup into individual bowls and garnish with the green onions. Serve.

GLUTEN FREE IF USING GLUTEN FREE FISH SAUCE

▸▸▸ **To make this soup vegetarian or vegan,** use water instead of the anchovy broth and omit the fish sauce.

KIMCHI GUK

김치국

Kimchi Soup

Serves 4

When napa cabbage kimchi is at its peak stage of ripeness, it is nicely crisp and tastes pleasantly sweet-sour. But when it has ripened to a point where it makes you pucker so much you no longer enjoy it right out of the container, repurpose the kimchi and its brine and use it to make this quick soup. Here its sourness will be an advantage, as the flavor will complement the seafood broth well.

1½ cups / 225g overripe napa kimchi,
    plus 3 tablespoons kimchi brine
    (and more brine as needed)

6 cups / 1.4L Anchovy and Dashi Broth
    (page 48) or store-bought

1 tablespoon Gahreun Mahneul /
    Blended Garlic (page 49)

1 cup / 120g sliced yellow onions
    (about ½ large onion)

4½ teaspoons fish sauce

2 green onions, green and white parts,
    sliced, for finishing

1 Slice the kimchi into small, thin pieces. Add the kimchi and brine to a medium pot, then add the broth and garlic. The broth should turn an orangish red; if it's lighter in color, add an additional tablespoon of the kimchi brine.

2 Turn the heat to high and boil until the kimchi pieces are soft, tender, and translucent, 15 to 20 minutes, then add the yellow onions and fish sauce. Boil for 5 to 10 minutes. As it boils, you may see some foam and impurities bubble to the surface of the soup; skim those off with a spoon as you see them and discard.

3 Add the green onions and turn off the heat. Serve.

GLUTEN-FREE IF USING GLUTEN-FREE FISH SAUCE

배추국

Soybean Soup with Cabbage

Serves 4

After I closed my restaurant, I began cooking more at home for my ninety-one-year-old mother. Baechooguk is her favorite dish, especially when she's not feeling well. This is a homey, salty, umami-filled soup, thanks to the doenjang (fermented soybean paste). And while you can use any quality doenjang you find at an Asian market, my secret is to combine the pastes from two brands, one from the brand CJ and the other from the brand Wang Foods, in equal parts. I always love making this soup for my mom, because I know she enjoys every bite, every slurp. This soup, she says, tastes like she's home.

- 6 cups / 1.4L Anchovy and Dashi Broth (page 48), homemade beef broth (pages 42 and 44), or store-bought
- 2 tablespoons doenjang (fermented soybean paste)
- 4½ teaspoons Gahreun Mahneul / Blended Garlic (page 49)
- 2 cups / 100g sliced (about 1 inch / 2.5cm) napa cabbage (about 1 head)
- 1 cup / 80g soybean sprouts, rinsed (optional)
- ½ cup / 70g diced yellow onions (about 1 small onion)
- 4½ teaspoons fish sauce
- 1½ teaspoons gochugaru (optional)
- 3 or 4 slices jalapeño (optional)
- ½ cup / 115g sliced green onions, green and white parts

1 Place a medium pot over high heat and add the broth. Bring to a boil, then add the doenjang and garlic and boil for 7 to 8 minutes. Add the cabbage and continue boiling for another 5 minutes, then add the sprouts (if using), yellow onions, fish sauce, gochugaru (if using), and jalapeño (if using). Boil just until the cabbage is tender, about another 10 minutes.

2 Add the green onions, ladle into bowls, and serve.

▸▸▸ **To make this dish vegetarian or vegan,** substitute the anchovy broth with vegetable broth or water and use soy sauce instead of the fish sauce.

MIYEOKGUK

미역국

Birthday Seaweed Soup

Serves 6 to 8

This seaweed soup is the equivalent of a birthday cake. Traditionally, this nourishing soup is prepared for new mothers to help them recover after childbirth; as a result, it's become a dish you have to have on the morning of your birthday. In fact, if you don't have it, it feels almost ominous—like bad luck is coming your way! To prepare the soup, I suggest using refrigerated rather than dried salted seaweed; it's available at Asian markets (I use the Wang Foods brand). The refrigerated version preserves the texture of the seaweed better than the dried version, and it cooks much faster. In either case, remember to soak and rinse the seaweed before cooking to soften the stems and remove the salt.

2 (10-oz / 282g) packages salted seaweed

½ lb / 225g ground beef, any cut but preferably rib eye or short rib trimmings

2½ tablespoons Gahreun Mahneul / Blended Garlic (page 49)

2 tablespoons fish sauce

1 teaspoon toasted sesame oil

2¼ teaspoons sea salt, plus more to taste

¼ teaspoon ground black pepper

1 Place the salted seaweed in a large bowl and cover with water. Let soak for about 1 hour, then rinse.

2 Place a large pot over high heat and add 1 cup / 240ml water, the seaweed, beef, garlic, fish sauce, sesame oil, salt, and black pepper. Boil the beef for about 10 minutes or until most of the liquid has evaporated. Add 8 cups / 1.9L water and boil for another 10 minutes. Add 7 more cups / 1.7L water and continue to boil until the seaweed is tender, 20 to 30 minutes. Taste, adding more salt if you'd like. Serve with rice.

GLUTEN-FREE IF USING GLUTEN-FREE FISH SAUCE

▸▸▸ **If you prefer to make this soup without beef, you have two options:**

- Replace the beef with 1 lb / 454g shucked fresh or frozen clams, oysters, or green or black mussels.

- Omit the beef and instead of the last 7 cups / 1.7L water, use Anchovy and Dashi Broth (page 48) and add ¼ cup / 30g sliced yellow onions.

DDUK MANDOO GUK
떡만두국

Rice Cake Soup with Dumplings

Serves 4

It is a family tradition to make this rice cake soup on New Year's Day. For every bowl you eat during the New Year, the saying goes, you "gain" one year of life, so, of course we have at least one bowl! We use packaged sliced rice cakes, which can be found in the refrigerated section of most Asian markets. We also add fresh pork mandoo (dumplings) to the soup, because, during the holiday, we always take the time to gather around the table and make them together. That said, frozen dumplings with your favorite filling are perfectly fine to use. In fact, I keep packaged mandoo in my freezer and a few extra packs of rice cakes in my fridge, so I can make this soup anytime throughout the year. It's a perfect quick dish to make when you want something comforting but don't feel like eating rice.

- 1 (24-oz / 680g) package Korean sliced rice cakes
- 2 large eggs
  Vegetable or other neutral oil, for the pan
- 8 cups / 1.9L Fast Beef Broth (page 42), with the marinated beef trimmings reserved
- 20 mandoo (dumplings with your preferred filling)
- 1 bunch green onions, green and white parts, sliced, for serving
- ½ teaspoon toasted sesame seeds (page 51), plus more to taste, for serving
- ¼ teaspoon ground black pepper, plus more to taste, for serving
- 1 sheet of roasted seaweed, crushed, or furikake, to taste, for serving

1 Place the rice cakes in a large bowl and add enough water to cover. Soak until they soften, 15 to 20 minutes.

2 Meanwhile, crack the eggs into a small bowl and whisk. Grease a small pan with the oil and place over medium heat. Pour the eggs into the pan and spread thin. Cook the eggs, undisturbed, until they're set, just a few minutes. Remove the eggs from the pan and cut into thin strips. Set aside.

3 Place a large pot over high heat, pour in the broth, and bring to a boil. Drop in the rice cakes and stir. Boil on high heat for 5 to 7 minutes, or until the rice cakes are tender.

4 Add the mandoo to the pot. When the mandoo begin to float, they're almost done. At that point, add the marinated beef trimmings and bring to a boil. I like to ensure the meat is cooked all the way through, so after adding the beef, I continue to cook the mandoo for a minute or two longer before turning off the heat.

5 To serve, ladle the soup into bowls and garnish each with the green onions, sesame seeds, black pepper, crushed roasted seaweed, and a few slices of egg. Taste and season with more sesame seeds, black pepper, and seaweed if needed.

OJINGEO GUK

오징어국

Spicy Squid Soup

Serves 4

This is one of my favorite soups. It brings me back to Korea, where we had access to incredibly fresh seafood, including squid, even in the winter. On those blustery winter days, I loved coming home to this soup simmering on the stove. The heat from the red pepper paste warmed me right up. The soup tastes even better the day after you make it, when the flavors have had a chance to meld, so I suggest making a large batch and setting aside a portion for later. My grandmother made this dish without soybean sprouts, which is why they're optional here; I like to add them because I like the texture and lightness they bring to the soup. If you do add the sprouts, note that they will discolor when the soup is reheated. They'll still be perfectly fine to eat, but if you'd prefer, finish eating any sprouts before you refrigerate the leftovers and add another handful before reheating. Serve with rice and kimchi for a satisfying meal.

- 2 lb / 900g whole squid, cleaned
- 1 lb / 450g mu / Korean radish (about 1 medium radish)
- ¼ cup plus 1 tablespoon / 100g Dadaegi / Seasoned Red Pepper Paste (page 49)
- 2 tablespoons Gahreun Mahneul / Blended Garlic (page 49)
- 1 tablespoon gochujang
- 1 cup / 120g sliced (about 1 inch / 2.5cm) yellow onions (about ½ large onion)
- 1 cup / 80g soybean sprouts, rinsed (optional)
- 1 tablespoon fish sauce
- 2 or 3 green onions, green and white parts, sliced

1 Score the squid in multiple places so it will be extra tender when cooked, then slice it into 1 by 1-inch / 2.5 by 2.5cm pieces. Set aside.

2 If the skin of the radish is especially thick and fibrous, peel and discard. Slice into 1-inch / 2.5cm pieces.

3 Place a medium pot over high heat and add 2½ qt / 2.4L water, the radishes, dadaegi, garlic, and gochujang. When the water comes to a boil, put the yellow onions, sprouts (if using), and squid into the pot and continue boiling until the squid is opaque and cooked through, 8 to 10 minutes. Add the fish sauce and green onions and boil for 5 to 10 minutes, during which time the green onions should soften and collapse. Portion the soup among the soup bowls and place them on the table for your guests.

SHIGEUMCHIGUK

시금치국

Soybean Soup with Spinach and Clams

Serves 4

A variety of Korean soups are made with doenjang, the fermented soybean paste you often find in tubs at Asian markets. Because its earthy flavor is so assertive, some people believe that soybean paste soups are heavy and overpowering; this recipe, though, shows how light a soybean paste soup can be. In addition to doenjang, I add miso paste to the broth. The sweet, mild, rounded flavor of the miso tempers the doenjang and further lifts the soup. (Both miso and doenjang are made from fermented soybeans, but miso incorporates a grain and a starter called koji to aid in its fermentation, unlike the process to make doenjang. The result is two soybean pastes with very different flavors.) Miso comes in white, yellow, and red varieties; the white is the mildest in flavor, while the red is the strongest. You can use any type for this recipe, though you may want to experiment with all three to see what you prefer. And while this soup is strong enough to stand on its own as a main dish, it's also clean, uplifting, and warm and complements most other dishes on the table well. As for the fillings, I generally use fresh clams, but frozen shell-on clams are fine, too. Rinse the frozen clams before using and soak them in water to partially defrost before adding them to the soup.

2 teaspoons sea salt

2 lb / 907g fresh baby clams

6 cups / 1.4L Anchovy and Dashi Broth (page 48) or store-bought

2 tablespoons doenjang (fermented soybean paste)

4½ teaspoons Gahreun Mahneul / Blended Garlic (page 49)

4½ teaspoons fish sauce

1 tablespoon red, white, or yellow miso paste

½ cup / 60g thinly sliced yellow onions (about ½ medium onion)

1½ teaspoons coarse gochugaru (optional)

6 cups / 120g spinach (2 to 3 bunches), washed well and drained

½ bunch green onions, green and white parts, sliced into 2-inch / 5cm pieces

1 Pour 4 cups / 950ml water into a large bowl and stir in the salt. Place the clams in the salted water and soak for 20 minutes, then drain. Scrub the clams to remove any remaining grit and sand, then rinse and set aside.

2 Place a medium pot over high heat and add the broth. Bring to a boil, then add the doenjang, garlic, fish sauce, and miso and boil for 7 to 8 minutes. Add the clams, yellow onions, and gochugaru (if you like a bit of heat) and boil until the clams open, 7 to 8 minutes (discard any clams that do not open). Then add the spinach and green onions and boil until the spinach is cooked through and tender, just a few minutes more.

MU GUK

무우국

Beef and Radish Soup

Serves 4

I like to think of mu guk as a Korean version of chicken noodle soup because it's light and so perfect when you're not feeling very well; indeed, mu (Korean radishes) have great digestive benefits. Since the soup doesn't use any spicy peppers, it is a great option for people, especially children, who prefer a non-spicy soup. It helps, too, that it is very easy to cook, especially if, like me, you often have scraps of beef and radishes in the fridge—you just put everything in a pot and boil!

⅓ to ½ lb / 150 to 225g short rib trimmings or any other fatty cut of beef, sliced into ¼-inch / 6mm pieces

¾ pound / 337g mu (Korean radish), peeled

1 medium yellow onion, cut into ⅛-inch / 3mm pieces

1 tablespoon Gahreun Mahneul / Blended Garlic (page 49)

1½ teaspoons fish sauce

1½ teaspoons sea salt

1½ teaspoons toasted sesame oil

½ teaspoon ground black pepper

2 or 3 green onions, green and white parts, cut into 1-inch / 2.5cm pieces, for garnish

1 In a medium bowl, soak the beef in 1 cup / 240ml cold tap water for 10 to 15 minutes, while you prepare the vegetables. Then rinse, dry, and set aside.

2 Slice the radish into 1-inch / 2.5cm square pieces approximately ¼-inch / 6mm in width (you should have about 2 cups / 220g). Add the radishes to a large pot.

3 Add the yellow onions to the pot, followed by the beef, garlic, fish sauce, salt, sesame oil, and black pepper. Turn the heat to high, mix well, and sauté until the beef is no longer pink. Pour in 5 cups / 1.2L water and boil until the radishes are tender, 15 to 20 minutes. Using a slotted spoon or ladle, skim the fat as it rises to the top (skimming the fat will keep the broth clear and impart a cleaner taste).

4 When the soup is ready, garnish with the green onions and serve.

GLUTEN-FREE IF USING GLUTEN-FREE FISH SAUCE

A Note from My Daughters

When I arrived in the United States from South Korea in the late 1970s, there were very few women who owned businesses, let alone businesses in Koreatown. By the time I had my two children, JJ and CJ, I had already ventured into running and owning my own business, knowing that it would require many personal sacrifices. But it was a risk I had to take because I believed that my work would contribute to a better life for my daughters.

I would often spend up to eighteen hours a day at the restaurant. It was my mother who watched my children, day in and day out. While customers celebrated special occasions at my restaurant and while my restaurant was growing up, I myself missed so many milestones in my daughters' lives. But I wanted my daughters to be proud of me and to understand what it meant for their mom—a woman, an immigrant, an entrepreneur—to work hard at something she loved. More than anything, I wanted to leave that legacy for them. With this cookbook, I wish to leave my daughters and the next generation of entrepreneurs a message: Do what matters to you. It will take hard work, but no matter the obstacles, if you pursue what you are most passionate and excited about, you will achieve success and happiness.

My daughters grew up with Beverly Soon Tofu. Not only is it part of me, it is also part of them. They wanted to leave a message, too, about what the restaurant meant to them. These are their words.

Mom ran the restaurant for thirty-four years in Koreatown, Los Angeles. We grew up in this restaurant. Throughout our childhood, we went with her to produce markets downtown to pick up the freshest ingredients for the restaurant. The restaurant was a frequent stop on the way home from school, so we'd wait patiently in the car while our mom and grandmom did what they needed to do. Many times, we went inside to say hello to the staff. They'd ask us if we had eaten, and if we hadn't, they'd give us whatever snacks, treats, or whole meals we wanted. They'd ask us about school and what we had learned that day. We would come to know many of them for decades, and they became like family. Outside of those visits, we didn't spend too much time in the restaurant, but it was always there, top of mind. The restaurant was Mom's third child, our youngest sibling, and the one who needed the most attention.

We grew up, went away to school, came back from school, and became adults. The restaurant was always there. We helped out in our free time, bussing tables, picking up the produce and supplies, translating official documents, and running the social media. Then during the pandemic, Mom needed our help urgently. Like so many businesses, the restaurant was struggling. Every day, money was going out and not much was coming in. We spent many weeks discussing the best next step, applying for what little COVID-19 relief was available. We downsized staff and updated our takeout menu. It was a heartbreaking, bittersweet, and emotional decision that we all made together, when we decided to close the restaurant in September of 2020.

At the time, we were definitely not the first pandemic casualty in Koreatown, so when we announced our plans to close, we had no expectations. But right after we made the announcement, we saw an outpouring of support from our loyal customers all across LA. To those who waited in the very long lines to get their last soon tofu order, please accept our apologies. We were not prepared for the volume of orders we received.

Those last ten days were all hands on deck, and even our friends came out to work shifts. We took time off from our everyday jobs to work the front of house and to say a proper farewell to my mom's restaurant.

We met loyal customers who had been coming to the restaurant since they were six or seven years old and now, in their forties, were coming back to say good-bye to Mom. She had been like a second mom to many of them and to so many others, too: those who had just moved to LA and didn't have a place where they felt comfortable; others who simply wanted a good warm meal. My mom instantly made them feel like family. Those last ten days were humbling, because we recognized what an enormous impact my mom had had on this community.

Since the restaurant closed, we have been helping our mom with this book. We are so grateful for this opportunity to start, literally, on a new chapter. This cookbook has given us a newfound appreciation for our mom, and it's been a true blessing to be able to have this time to cook with her. (And, quite frankly, we have enjoyed seeing her finally take a break!) Having her share what these recipes mean to her and, of course, show us how to make so many of the dishes we grew up eating, has been a chance for us to appreciate, savor, and celebrate her food. Her sohn-mat.

The food at Beverly Soon Tofu was warm, homey, and delicious. It was a small restaurant with ten tables—bustling, old-school Korean American. It was a perfect expression of our mom: her hard work, her dedication, her sacrifices, her love for cooking for others, her nurturing of community. Our mom put thirty-four years of her life into the restaurant. To our sister, Beverly Soon Tofu, thank you for all you have provided us and our family. We hope that your memory will live on in this cookbook.

Resources

Below is a list of sources for a wide selection of ingredients and supplies and for learning more about Korean and Korean American culture.

Groceries and Pantry Staples

These are my preferred places to shop for groceries and pantry supplies.

NATIONAL MARKETS

H Mart
H Mart is a national Korean supermarket chain with a wide variety of produce, meat, seafood, and pantry staples.
hmart.com

99 Ranch
Although it doesn't specialize in Korean products, 99 Ranch offers a wide range of Asian ingredients, and most of what you will need to cook from this book can be found there. They have locations in California, Oregon, Washington, Nevada, Arizona, Texas, Virginia, Maryland, New Jersey, New York, and Massachusetts.
99ranch.com

Hannam Chain Market
Hannam has locations throughout Southern California as well as in New Jersey. You can see all their locations on their website.
hannamchain.com

WHOLESALE MARKET

HL Foods
2920 W. Pico Blvd.
Los Angeles, CA 90006

If you're in Los Angeles, HL Foods is an excellent resource. It is a wholesale market and supplier with many Korean and other Asian items available in bulk.

LOCAL KOREAN MARKETS

Los Angeles is home to the largest Koreatown in the country, but there are Koreatowns all over the United States, as well as small, independent Korean and Asian markets outside of those neighborhoods. I encourage you to seek them out and support them.

ONLINE SOURCES

Weee!
Weee! is an online market specializing in Asian and Hispanic products. It ships nationwide.
sayweee.com/en

H&Y

Based in Brooklyn, this Korean grocer ships nationwide.

hanyangmart.com

Amazon

Amazon stocks many Korean pantry staples, including items from major Korean brands.

amazon.com

Kitchen Equipment, Supplies, and Tableware

Many of the ceramics featured in our photographs were supplied by Insuk Son, a ceramicist based in Southern California. You can find more of her work at insceramics.com or on Instagram @insceramics.

H Mart and many Korean markets are great resources for cooking supplies. You often can find ttukbaegi, dolsots, kimchi containers, green onion slicers, and other kitchenware and equipment in their housewares sections.

The following sources offer a great selection of cooking equipment and supplies for making soon tofu, kimchi, and other Korean dishes:

Home Shopping World

Home Shopping World is located in Los Angeles but ships worldwide.

hswusa.com

Amazon

Many Korean resellers offer ttukbaegi, dolsots, and other supplies and tableware on Amazon.

amazon.com

If you're in Los Angeles, these are great destinations for kitchen supplies:

Lotte Kitchen World

1589 W. Washington Blvd.
Los Angeles, CA 90007

lottekitchen.wixsite.com/lottekitchen

Kitchen Plus

3250 Olympic Blvd., Suite 113
Los Angeles, CA 90006

kitchenplus.business.site

Kim's Home Center

2940 W. Olympic Blvd.
Los Angeles, CA 90006

kimshome.com

Culture

The University of Southern California's Korean Heritage Library is an excellent resource for information about Korean and Korean American culture. Its wealth of resources includes an online digital archive in addition to an extensive physical collection.

Doheny Memorial Library

University of Southern California
3550 Trousdale Parkway
Los Angeles, CA 90089-1825

libraries.usc.edu/locations/ east-asian-library/ korean-heritage-library

Acknowledgments

Thanks to:

TIEN NGUYEN, the coauthor of this book, who captured everything I wanted to say and more! I honestly didn't think I had a lot to say, but you got every story I never knew I wanted to tell aloud for everyone to read! I appreciate your patience and your humor on every Zoom call, listening to countless hours of me telling you the weekly price of green onions at the market!

MICHELE CRIM of Miller Bowers Griffin Literary Management LLC, my literary agent, who approached me in September 2020 when the pandemic forced us to close the restaurant and encouraged me to write a cookbook to memorialize the beautiful trajectory of my restaurant and my cooking. I cannot thank you enough for connecting me to all the amazing people who contributed to making this book a reality and enabling me to have a written legacy for my daughters and my granddaughter.

JENNY WAPNER of Hardie Grant, our editor and publisher, for believing in this book and in my vision for it. I so appreciate your expertise and the tireless hours you spent developing and guiding our manuscript.

CAROLYN INSLEY of Hardie Grant, who provided invaluable editorial support, and **DOLORES YORK,** whose copyedits and attention to language and detail made our recipes and stories ever stronger.

TONI TAJIMA, who showcased my recipes so beautifully with her design.

RICK POON, our amazing photographer, who saw eye to eye with me on the direction of the photography. Through your lens, you captured my dishes exactly how I imagined them to be. I am beyond amazed at your attention to detail and your focus on the feel of the book.

DIEP TRAN for taking the time to be a part of our team and lending us your vast cooking experience and creativity during all of our photo shoots.

INSUK SON, the talented ceramicist whose pieces really spoke to the aesthetic we were striving for. Thank you for your generosity.

JESSICA WANG, MATTEO MAZZIE, and **MELISA HANPARSUN** for lending us beautiful dishware and other props from your own kitchens for our photo shoots.

HAENG NAM CHU of Lotte Kitchen World and **SOON MO HONG** of Hannam Chain Market, for your generosity and for supplying the restaurant for so many years.

Our recipe testers **BRETT GABBY, CASEY CURTIS, CATHERINE CHANG, EMILY WADA, JESSICA GHURABI, JESSICA STERN, JILL ADKINS, KEVIN WEE, KYUNG KIM, LINDA NAKAGAWA, NA YOUNG MA, NY LEE, PHIL SHIN, ROBERT GILBERT, SHARON MARUYA, SHINAE KIM, STELLA LEE, SUSIE KIM, TONY LEE, WENDY DANG, AND WINNIE HO.** I am so grateful for your feedback, enthusiasm, and willingness to try out our recipes.

JOY KIM and **SUJEONG KWON,** at the Korean Heritage Library at USC, for their research assistance.

CAROLINE MARUYA, MIKE KIM, and **RAFFI GHURABI.** Along with my daughters, you were part of my support system during this entire process, and I cannot thank you enough.

JENNY KIM, for capturing and sharing wonderful memories of the restaurant and my family over the years with her photography.

My sister, **MEUNG SUN PARK,** who helped record the recipes even when it meant staying up all night to write out all the measurements; my mother, **MYONG SOON YUN,** who supported me throughout the life of the restaurant and helped me raise my two daughters; my sister-in-law, **YOUNG YUN,** who did a little of everything to make sure we were on track to get this cookbook done; my aunt **MYONG JU SOHN,** who always has been not just an aunt but also a confidante who guided me through good times and bad; and my grandma, **OH BOONG YI,** who inspired my passion for cooking when I was a young girl.

Lastly, I want to thank **MY TWO DAUGHTERS, JJ AND CJ,** for standing with me through all of this and sharing in this amazing journey. I dedicate this cookbook to you two.

If time, experience, and opportunity in Koreatown Los Angeles have taught me anything, it is to remain in the moment: to savor it, learn from it, and appreciate it. Writing this cookbook has given me the opportunity to reflect on the last three decades in a way I have not before, and my appreciation for those moments has only deepened. Thank you to my loyal customers and thank you to the readers of this book. I hope you will enjoy my recipes and make many delicious meals from them.

Index